Beating Dyspraxia
with a Hop, Skip and a Jump

1800 8435575
91463? Bot ED

PLUS LOAN
— permanently
    disabled.
Federal Family Ed Loan Program

of related interest

Caged in Chaos
A Dyspraxic Guide to Breaking Free
Victoria Biggs
Foreword by Jo Todd
Illustrated by Sharon Tsang
ISBN 978 1 84905 474 4
eISBN 978 0 85700 873 2

Can I tell you about Dyspraxia?
A guide for friends, family and professionals
Maureen Boon
Illustrated by Imogen Hallam
Part of the Can I tell you about...? series
ISBN 978 1 84905 447 8
eISBN 978 0 85700 824 4

Understanding Dyspraxia
A Guide for Parents and Teachers
Maureen Boon
Part of the JKP Essentials series
ISBN 978 1 84905 069 2
eISBN 978 0 85700 259 4

Understanding Motor Skills in Children with Dyspraxia, ADHD, Autism, and Other Learning Disabilities
A Guide to Improving Coordination
Lisa A. Kurtz
Part of the JKP Essentials series
ISBN 978 1 84310 865 8
eISBN 978 1 84642 672 8

Beating
Dyspraxia

with a Hop, Skip and a Jump

A Simple Exercise Program to Improve
Motor Skills at Home and School

Revised Edition

Geoff Platt

Jessica Kingsley *Publishers*
London and Philadelphia

Extracts from Kirby and Drew 2003 on p.19–20, 24 and 27–28
are reproduced by permission of David Fulton
Table 3.2 from N.A. Ratamess 2008 on p.79 is reproduced by permission of Human Kinetics
Extract from Schmidt and Wrisberg 2008 on p.86–7 is reproduced by permission of Human Kinetics
Extract from Macintyre on p.88–89 is reproduced by permission of David Fulton
Extracts from R. Martens 1981 on p.128-131 are reproduced by permission of Human Kinetics

This revised edition published in 2015
by Jessica Kingsley Publishers
73 Collier Street
London N1 9BE, UK
and
400 Market Street, Suite 400
Philadelphia, PA 19106, USA

www.jkp.com

First edition published by Jessica Kingsley Publishers, 2011

Library of Congress Cataloging in Publication Data
Platt, Geoff, 1955-
Beating dyspraxia with a hop, skip and a jump : a simple exercise program to improve motor skills at
home and school / Geoff Platt. -- Revised edition.
pages cm
Includes bibliographical references and index.
ISBN 978-1-84905-560-4 (alk. paper)
1. Apraxia--Exercise therapy. 2. Motor ability in children. 3. Movement disorders in children. I. Title.
RJ496.A63P53 2015
618.92'8552--dc23
2014026465

British Library Cataloguing in Publication Data
A CIP catalogue record for this book is available from the British Library

ISBN 978 1 84905 560 4
eISBN 978 0 85700 948 7

Printed and bound in Great Britain by Bell & Bain Ltd, Glasgow

Contents

Acknowledgements

I would like to start by thanking the man who has done the most to make this work happen, Dr John Sproule.

The research would not have been possible without the support of a number of schools in Croydon and I would like to express my appreciation for their support and assistance.

Gresham Primary School

Keston Primary School

Oval Primary School

Rowdown Primary School

Wolsey Primary School

I would also like to thank Dr Nikos Papadakis, who collaborated on the entropy research, Professor Mohsen Shafizadeh, who collaborated with the movement skills research and Mrs Signa Ashdown, who came to my assistance on several cold winter days when there were just too many children for me alone!

Finally, thank you to my family, for their love and support and their understanding for those times during my research when I was not around.

Preface

A few years ago I entered the local fun run with my 13-year-old daughter. During the race I noticed that she was experiencing difficulties in her running style and, after the race, I mentioned this to my wife. We discussed the best way to address the problem – my wife wanted to take our daughter to see our GP but I wanted to take her to see a friend who was a physiotherapist. In due course the GP referred my daughter to see an orthopaedic surgeon at our local general hospital; I took my daughter to see the physiotherapist. The surgeon recommended immediate surgery; the physiotherapist recommended a course of physiotherapy. I learned an important lesson: we all run to our own specialisms when dealing with problems.

So it is with dyspraxia. Hundreds of books have been written on the subject, by authors who were sufferers, parents of sufferers, teachers, doctors, physiotherapists, occupational therapists, etc. The authors recommend all sorts of solutions, ranging from drills designed to practise every life skill required by a five year old, to visual skills exercises. Few of these 'solutions' have any measurable effect, and even fewer have a lasting effect. However, it is now more than 25 years since a direct correlation between dyspraxia and a lack of muscular strength was proved and since strength training was proved to reduce the symptoms of dyspraxia by 72 per cent, making it the only universal intervention that has been proved to work.

Between 1989 and 2001, an Australian sports physiologist by the name of Annette Raynor researched strength as an issue for children with dyspraxia and published two papers on the results of her research. She showed that there was a correlation between children with dyspraxia and children with poor isometric leg strength and showed that this was linked to poor muscle activation and co-activation.

In 1997 two superintendent physiotherapists in London, Michelle Lee and Graham Smith, decided to review a number of interventions that were being used across London hospitals to assist children with dyspraxia (Lee and Smith 1998). Parents, identifying that their children were experiencing movement difficulties, were taking their children to see the family doctor who was referring the children to the local hospital. At the hospital the doctors, lacking any firm guidance, were referring the children to physiotherapists or occupational therapists for support. The occupational therapists identified tasks that were troubling the children and then set about practising them. The physiotherapists had attempted a wide range of interventions and this review was an attempt to identify what worked and what did not.

Lee and Smith found that the best results were achieved when each child's movement skills were individually assessed and a professional judgement made about the likely causes so that an individualized strength training program could be designed. This program was performed five times each week under parental guidance, and once under the guidance of the physiotherapist in order to provide support for the parent and child.

In this way, Lee and Smith identified that they were able to achieve a 72 per cent reduction in the symptoms of dyspraxia experienced by the children after only eight weeks.

Unfortunately, the cost of the intensive employment of specialist paediatric physiotherapists over a period of almost six months was found to be prohibitive and this intervention appears to have almost completely lapsed.

A number of observers have identified that children with dyspraxia have weak muscles, particularly in their fingers, hands and wrists. Despite these observations, and the fact that strength has been identified as improving the symptoms of those with cerebral palsy, whilst dyspraxia has been referred to as *minimal cerebral palsy*, only four pieces of research into the effects of strength and strength training on dyspraxia appear to have been published.

I decided to conduct my own research and to design an exercise program that was simpler and more closely related to a child's natural play, which required only minimal equipment to perform, and which required only minimal, unqualified supervision. My results matched those of the previous researchers and I decided to publish my findings in a book as well as in peer-previewed journals, in an attempt to spread the word and change attitudes to the condition.

But 72 per cent is not 100 per cent. Children with dyspraxia avoid participation in sport and school Physical Education (PE) lessons. None of us like to embarrass ourselves by showing others our weaknesses, preferring instead to show off our talents. As a result, children with dyspraxia fail to develop movement skills in the same way that other children do.

Praxis is the process by which we plan our movements. It is the process by which cricketers decide which way to run, how fast to run and what they need to do with their hands to catch a ball on the boundary. It is the process by which hurdlers decide how many steps they need to take and how long each step needs to be, in order to take the next hurdle comfortably. It is the process by which a child coordinates his or her hand and mouth so that an ice cream goes to his or her mouth, rather than to his or her forehead.

The second phase of the intervention in this book is aimed at assisting children with dyspraxia in a series of exercises designed to assist them in their praxis skills and so assist them to catch up with their peers, who have been actively participating in sport throughout their lives.

This book provides parents, sports coaches and teachers with methods to help children with dyspraxia to improve their movement skills. It will also encourage further research into an area that has provided positive results and will help to ensure that strength and muscle training are not overlooked for another ten years.

Part I

The Background

Chapter 1

What Is Dyspraxia?

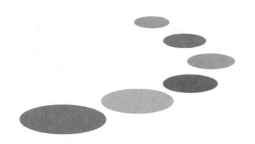

Experts agree that over the period of the last century there has been a loss of movement skills among some children, so that a group now exists who may be described as clumsy and in need of support. They may knock into furniture, have difficulty writing and drawing and quickly gain a reputation for misbehaving.

These difficulties are usually first identified at school where children are seen by teachers and compared with others of a similar age and background, and judgements can more easily be made than at home, where the children are seen in isolation within their family.

Of course, schools, like every other part of our society, are changing. Pressure from the government to raise standards in literacy, numeracy and science have compelled head teachers to increase the amount of time that children spend in the classroom and thereby reduce the time that they spend outside studying nature, exploring our environment and simply moving around freely.

Classrooms now contain a wide range of valuable, electronic equipment ranging from computers, televisions and DVD players to electronic whiteboards; some schools even provide each individual child with his or her own laptop computer on which to do schoolwork. With all this valuable equipment in the classroom it is clear to see that there is no room for clumsy children running around and knocking over the furniture, and that strict discipline needs to be enforced.

Teachers are caring people who work in teams in schools and when they began noticing that there was a problem with the movement skills of their children they started to talk about it with their colleagues and then, when they found no easy solution to the problem, to start writing papers that were published to wider groups of fellow teachers and other professionals. The professionals included in these discussions about children with movement difficulties include:

- teachers

- physical education specialists

- special educational needs coordinators (SENCOs)

- educational psychologists

- social workers

- doctors/paediatricians

- orthopaedic surgeons

- speech and language therapists

- occupational therapists

- physiotherapists.

As the debate widened there was a need to give the condition a name and some of the names that teachers and other professionals gave the condition included, according to Boon:

- dyspraxia

- clumsy child syndrome

- developmental agnosia and apraxia

- developmental coordination disorder (DCD)

- learning difficulties/disabilities/disorders

- minimal cerebral palsy

- minimal cerebral dysfunction

- minimal brain dysfunction

- minimal motor dysfunction

- motor learning difficulties

- neurodevelopmental dysfunction

- perceptual/perceptuo-motor dysfunction

- physical awkwardness

- specific learning difficulties

- sensori-motor dysfunction.

(Boon 2010, p.9)

The labels that were selected are interesting in that they reflect the way in which the condition was viewed. In the UK the term that has stuck is 'dyspraxia'. *Praxis* is the function by which we plan movement. If you want to catch a ball that is coming towards you, you need first to judge its distance from you, its trajectory and its speed. You then need to work out a way to get yourself underneath it as it comes to earth, by running towards it and placing your hands together under the ball and clamping them together at the exact second that the ball arrives between them.

If you were asked to explain these calculations on paper, few of us could do so, but most of us are able to do these calculations in our head and catch the ball at the same time! The name dyspraxia reflects a belief that the movement difficulties reflect an inability in those with the condition to perform this planning and therefore, to execute these movements.

In the United States, the condition is sometimes called 'developmental coordination disorder' (or DCD) to reflect that the condition is seen as a problem of growing children failing to make progress at the same rate as their peers. The word 'coordination' leaves the cause of the problem open to wider discussion than the UK equivalent of 'praxis'. However, 'dyspraxia' and 'developmental coordination disorder' are generally understood to be interchangeable terms and will be taken to refer to the same condition in this book.

Labelling a condition has the advantage that it acknowledges that a problem exists and assists in making applications for funding for research into a named condition rather than a more abstract problem. Unfortunately, it may also be seen as an excuse for poor behaviour by some families and as a justification for failing to attempt to raise standards. According to Kirby and Drew (2003) a label can mean:

- Acknowledgement for the parent of worries and concerns, and confirmation of the condition: allows others to see the parent as not just 'another over-anxious parent'.

- The provision of funds or services for the child.

- The provision of a cohort of individuals with signs and symptoms that may be useful for research.

- Allowing individuals working with the child to read up around the condition and consider what type of support is required.

- It may be used in legal cases as a reference point to consider one child's support compared to others.

- It may be used to plan service delivery or for baseline assessment and in-school remediation programmes.

- It may suggest negative connotations and may mean that individuals who come into contact with the child have preconceived ideas about the strengths and difficulties based on their experience of others with the same label they have come into contact with, who could even have been atypical.

- Placing children in very small boxes and not seeing them from all perspectives – this may lead to missing a diagnosis.

- The child perhaps ends up with many labels but not the right type of help.

- The child then being 'tattooed' for life with what they can't do rather than what they can do.

- One label does not carry as much weight as another; for instance, medical labels may seem more important than educational ones (e.g. epilepsy versus dyslexia).

(Kirby and Drew 2003, pp.1–2)

At the same time as the researchers were labelling the condition they set out to list the symptoms of the disorder that they were witnessing. The most complete list of symptoms is grouped into lists below.

The areas affected are:

- gross motor skills (these involve skills such as running, jumping and throwing)

- fine motor skills (these include tasks undertaken whilst sitting at a desk such as writing, drawing, putting pegs in a board)

- speech and language

- social skills

- attention and concentration

- learning

- visual motor skills.

The primary problems include:

- low muscle tone

- weak hands and fingers

- fast fatigue of the muscles

- poor joint stability

- inability to conceptualize movement, particularly across their midline

- inability to execute movements, particularly across their midline

- poor coordination

- poor balance

- poor attention

- inability to screen out the non-relevant

- poor proprioceptive feedback (poor awareness of own movement)

- poor tactile feedback (poor sensitivity to touch)

- overall lack of inhibition in the central nervous system (over-excitement of the central nervous system)

- hyperactivity

- poor eye movements.

The secondary problems of dyspraxia are:

- lack of confidence

- poor self-esteem

- refusal to participate

- avoidance

- frustration

- unhappiness

- loneliness

- becoming withdrawn

- acting the clown.

When the researchers had agreed that there was a problem that needed to be addressed, labelled it and drawn up a list of symptoms, they set about writing a definition for the disorder. A number of other professionals from a range of other specialisms have also attempted to define the condition. Although a number of definitions have been written, the one that is most authoritative and widely accepted is the one published by the American Psychiatric Association (APA) in the most recent version of their *Diagnostic and Statistical Manual of Mental Disorders* (DSM-5).

Their definition is more remarkable for what it excludes rather than what it includes. It lists the essential features of the condition without attempting to list or even suggest what the other features may include. It limits diagnosis of the condition to those cases where 'the impairment significantly interferes with academic achievement or activities of daily living'. Most significantly, the definition makes no attempt to set out the causes of the condition, preferring instead to exclude a number of possible causes.

The variation in the symptoms from child to child has prompted a number of researchers to speculate that there may be a number of varieties of the condition, each focusing on a particular skill. The best distinction between types of dyspraxia as linked to the areas affected is found in Maureen Boon's book:

- verbal dyspraxia

- sensory integrative dysfunction

- ideational dyspraxia (difficulty in planning the best way to undertake a movement task)

- ideomotor dyspraxia (difficulty in converting planned movement into actual movement).

(Boon 2010, p.11)

Previously, she had also included:

- oral dyspraxia

- occulomotor dyspraxia (difficulty in coordinating vision and movement in a task)

- constructional dyspraxia (difficulty in building solutions)

- dressing dyspraxia.

(Boon 2002, p.12)

Several researchers have recognized that the causes and symptoms of dyspraxia vary and have attempted to differentiate between various types of the condition. Most have simply compared the results of a range of movement tests in order to find similarities and differences between children. Some have watched the children in order to identify differences and others have attempted to understand the causes of the children's problems and differentiate that way. This concept of identifying various types of dyspraxia may prove useful if it diminishes the expectation that a single universal cause and intervention may be discovered for dyspraxia and instead focuses attention onto several different causes that each require a separate intervention that needs to be identified.

This already complex situation is further complicated by the fact that at the same time that dyspraxia was being identified and investigated other researchers were looking into a range of conditions that they referred to as 'specific learning difficulties'. The term relates to problems identified in an educational setting usually in reading, writing, spelling and number work, sometimes called the 'developmental tasks' of the school-age child. They include:

- dyslexia (difficulties with spelling and reading);

- Asperger's Syndrome (difficulties making friends, seeing things literally);

- dyspraxia (difficulties with ball skills, poor handwriting at speed, difficulty with dressing);

- Attention Deficit Hyperactivity Disorder (difficulty concentrating when noisy, easily distracted, impulsive);

- deficit of attention and motor perception (difficulty in paying attention and movement control);

- dysgraphia (difficulty in writing);

- dyscalculia (difficulty with sums).

(Kirby and Drew 2003, p.2)

Who gets dyspraxia?

It would be easy to write off children with dyspraxia as being stupid, but this is not the case. In fact, the reverse is true, and those with specific learning disorders are more likely to be of above average intelligence and their difficulties unexpected when their general intellectual ability is taken into account. It has also been noticed that those with a specific learning disorder are unlikely to suffer from only one of these conditions. There is a debate currently taking place within the scientific community as to whether these people are all suffering with the same condition of 'specific learning difficulties' that is manifested in a range of symptoms that vary from person to person, or whether each condition listed above has a separate cause and a separate list of symptoms.

The incidence of dyspraxia

Most researchers estimate the incidence of dyspraxia at between 5 and 10 per cent of the population, with three times as many boys as girls affected. To put these numbers in perspective, this means that if the average class contains 32 children, there could be as many as four children with dyspraxia in the class. If the class is equally divided between boys and girls then one girl out of 16 is likely to have dyspraxia and three boys out of 16 are likely to have the condition.

Symptoms of dyspraxia

There are a range of symptoms for dyspraxia but none of them is essential for a diagnosis. The skills of those with the disorder may vary from hour-to-hour and from day-to-day, depending on their level of exhaustion and their ability to concentrate, making diagnosis difficult.

Anecdotal evidence suggests that the symptoms of dyspraxia start shortly after conception (Kirby and Drew 2003, p.19). Research (Kirby and Drew 2003, p.20) has shown that movement by the baby in the womb starts at six weeks and after that, mothers report that babies in the sixth week of pregnancy, who later experience movement difficulties in childhood, have been identified by their lack of movement in the womb at this time. This would therefore mean that these problems occur very early in our development, but this requires further research in order to confirm the facts. Some researchers (Brookes 2007a, 2007b) have attempted to include cases in which the symptoms have been said to develop later in life in their research into dyspraxia, but these are outside the usual definitions as they cannot be described as developmental. Such cases often have their basis in some traumatic event and as such probably have a different physiological basis – their inclusion could therefore confuse research into the causes and treatment of the condition.

The symptoms of dyspraxia diminish in both number and significance as the child grows up and continues to develop. Most children are able to achieve acceptable standards of performance in the key skills of walking, running and talking just within the 'normal' time span, although their performance never quite reaches the same level as that of the average child, and some symptoms persist into adolescence and even into adulthood. As well as continuing to develop, the child also learns coping strategies to deal with his or her difficulties, such as avoiding PE classes or growing up and leaving school so that he or she is not required to take part in sporting activities.

Tests for dyspraxia

Serious problems exist in designing a test for a condition in which the symptoms vary from child-to-child and from day-to-day and even from hour-to-hour and when no symptom is essential for the diagnosis of the condition, and where no cause of the condition has been accepted.

A number of tests have been designed in order to identify those children with movement skills problems. These include:

- Denver Developmental Screening Test (Frankenburg and Dodds 1967; Frankenburg *et al.* 1990)

- Bayley Scales of Infant Development (Bayley 1969)

- Peabody Developmental Motor Scales (Folio and Fewell 2000)

- Schedule of Growing Skills II (Bellman *et al.* 1996)

- Purdue Perceptual Motor Survey (Roach and Kephart 1966)

- Bruininks-Oseretsky Test of Motor Proficiency (Bruininks 1978)

- Fundamental Movement Pattern Assessment Instrument (McClenaghan 1976; McClenaghan and Gallahue 1978; Gallahue and Ozmun 1995)

- Developmental Sequence of Fundamental Motor Skills Inventory (Seefeldt and Haubenstricker 1976; Haubenstricker, Seefeldt, Fountain and Sapp 1981)

- Test of Gross Motor Development (Ulrich 1985)

- Ohio State University Scale of Intra-Gross Motor Assessment (Loovis and Ersing 1976)

- Basic Motor Ability Tests – Revised (Arnheim and Sinclair 1979)

- Movement ABC Battery for Children (Henderson and Sugden 1992)

- Pediatric Evaluation of Disability Inventory (PEDI) (Haley, Coster, Ludlow, Haltiwanger and Andrellos 1992)

- The School Function Assessment (Coster, Deeney, Haltiwanger and Haley 1998)

- Ecological Task Analysis (Davis and Burton 1991)

- Examination of the Child with Minor Neurological Dysfunction (Touwen 1979)

- Kinaesthetics and Sensitivity Test (Laszlo and Bairstow 1985)

- The Abilities of Young Children Test (Griffiths 1970)

- Southern California Sensory Integration Test (Ayres 1972)

(Kirby and Drew 2003, pp.57–58)

In the UK there is an almost universal acceptance of the Movement Assessment Battery for Children Test (usually abbreviated to the Movement ABC). The test was designed by two researchers (Henderson and Sugden) into education from the University of Leeds in 1992 and the following photographs show a little of how it works.

Table 1.1: Movement ABC photo album

Manual dexterity (fine motor skills)

Shifting pegs by rows This boy is moving pegs across the board. For this task, we test how well the children perform with both their dominant and non-dominant hands.	**Threading nuts on bolt** Here the boy is threading three nuts onto a bolt. We give him two attempts at this.	**Flower trail** For this task, the child is asked to draw between two lines. Our subject focuses intently on his drawing.

cont.

Ball skills (throw and catch)	
Two-hand catch Here we throw the ball against the wall and catch it. 	**Throwing bean bag into box** One of the tasks in our Movement ABC test is to throw a bean bag into a box.

Dynamic balance		
Hopping in squares One hop in each square. No more; no less.	**Ball balance** 'All I have to do is keep this tennis ball on top of this board? No problem.'	**One-board balance** 'WHOA!!!!' As is demonstrated in this picture, it is quite difficult to stand on one foot on this block for very long. Don't worry folks, no children were injured in the making of this picture.

In the United States of America there is an almost universal acceptance of the Bruininks-Oseretsky Test of Motor Proficiency (Bruininks 1978); other countries use other tests. A comparison of the two named tests found significant differences in the results and a correlation of only 0.80, indicating that neither was better than the other, but rather that the best results were achieved by undertaking both tests (Crawford, Wilson and Dewey 2001). Other researchers compared the results generated by three popular methods of testing children's movement skills, the Test of Motor Proficiency, the Test of Motor Impairment (TOMI) and the judgement of teachers found that each procedure identified a different set of children as poorly coordinated (Crawford *et al.* 2001; Keogh 1982; Sugden and Wright 1998).

My discussions with those regularly performing assessments of children referred to them by schools, due to their movement skills difficulties, indicate that a number of problems exist with the current testing arrangements. The cost of testing kits at around £750/$1200 has meant that most counties in the UK and equivalent regions in the USA have purchased just one kit, thereby limiting the potential number of tests to be performed. This also generally means that the kit remains with one assessor, thus reducing the opportunity for other assessors to gain the necessary knowledge and experience of using it. If the kit were cheaper then it should be possible for counties to purchase more and train more assessors and it might even be possible to encourage some schools to purchase their own kits and train their own assessors, with the possibility of universal screening taking place.

The limited availability of the testing kits, together with the need for statutory assessments, means that assessors have to visit schools for individual tests. Each assessment takes half a working day to complete. On top of that, there is travelling time to the school, time spent meeting and greeting colleagues and making essential rooming arrangements and setting up and putting away the testing equipment so each test takes a full working day to complete. This limits testing to a maximum of five children per week, and with other responsibilities taken into consideration, usually fewer. Several authors (e.g. Kirby and Drew 2003) have indicated that a number of additional tests are required for a full diagnosis, with one group of experienced researchers and authors recommending that the tests need to be repeated by class teachers, PE teachers, special educational specialists, speech and language therapists and others. They also suggest using the tests in a wide range of settings whilst the child uses reading, writing, speaking and other skills which will, of course, considerably extend the time taken to complete the diagnosis.

Another complication in assessing children suspected of having dyspraxia is that diagnosis tends to take place in two ways. When *teachers* identify a problem they refer the child to the school's SENCO who will assess the child and then refer the child to an educational psychologist for a comprehensive assessment. If *parents* are troubled by their child's movement difficulties they will take the child to see their doctor. If the GP is satisfied that there is a problem he or she will refer the child to a paediatric specialist at their local hospital.

These specialists possess widely different knowledge and experience and this will be reflected in their assessment of the condition. When a child is assessed by a doctor, he or she will generally accept anecdotal evidence of movement skills problems from the parent. The doctor will, however, have the clear ability to consider the incidence of any other medical condition which may be present and will devote all available time to considering this issue.

An educational psychologist conducting an assessment will generally undertake a full and careful assessment as set down in his or her training. An educational psychologist's ability to consider alternative medical diagnoses, must, of necessity, be limited when compared to that of the doctor.

In the UK a code of practice has been established for the assessment of children with movement skills difficulties (see Figure 1.1). The code of practice provided for communication between parents and teachers, referral to school SENCOs and professional assessment by an educational psychologist. Unfortunately, as the code is a Department for Education document (2001), parents are generally unaware of it unless they communicate with a teacher and therefore many parents, identifying movement skills difficulties in their child, take him or her to see their doctor, who then makes a diagnosis in his or her own way.

The teaching and medical professions have vastly different areas of knowledge and expertise and few doctors have the training, experience or equipment necessary to carry out a Movement ABC test on a child brought to them by a concerned parent.

The Movement ABC test is almost 20 years old. It is universally accepted in the UK as the official and best test for dyspraxia, despite the extensive list of weaknesses that have been revealed in the literature. Its greatest strength is that it allows children with movement difficulties to be assessed in a range of activities. This enables a trained and experienced assessor to identify the specific problems that underlie the difficulties that the child is experiencing and which have been identified by parents and/or teachers. The test also allows an element of objectivity to be introduced into the assessment, which is essential if support and assistance are to be provided to the child from a publicly funded service, such as Education or Health.

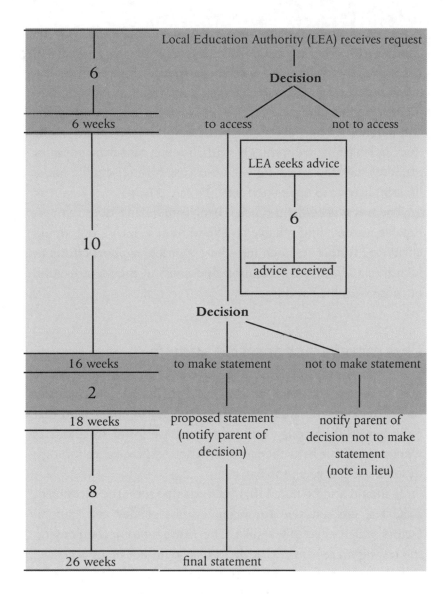

Figure 1.1: Process of assessment from Code of Practice for Special Educational Needs
(Department for Education 2001)

Errors in diagnosis have very serious consequences for the children concerned. A child with dyspraxia who is missed will not receive the support and assistance that he or she deserves, may be disciplined for accidents that occur as a result of undiagnosed movement difficulties and may be considered a failure by teachers and parents. A child diagnosed with dyspraxia, when he or she does not have it, will struggle with the pre-conceived ideas of teaching staff and will be given an excuse for indiscipline and a lifelong licence to under-perform.

There is a need for a quick, cheap, simple and objective test capable of providing reliable and valid results. Such a test would encourage further research into the condition, support efforts to identify an effective intervention and assist in the identification of those with the condition.

Dyspraxia across the world

Dyspraxia is only recognized in certain countries, such as the UK, USA and Australia, and in Western Europe. In countries still struggling with AIDS and HIV it is easy to understand that movement skills among children are not a priority. In countries where schools are held outside and without expensive technology, dyspraxia is less of a problem.

It should also be noted that the tests that form the Movement ABC test are sensitive to social, ethnic, gender and cultural factors which affect the results. The instructions accompanying the testing kit set down that the tests should not be of practised skills but rather of new activities outside of the child's experience – or raw skills. Indeed, the instructions generally call for the assessor to permit one practice attempt for each activity so as to allow the subject an opportunity to become familiar with the activity and the equipment.

One of the tests for a child aged between eight and ten years is the two-hand catch (see page 30). This requires the child to stand eight feet away from a flat wall and throw a tennis ball against the wall and catch it without allowing it to bounce or touch his or her arms or chest. Most boys born within the Indian sub-continent will score ten out of ten for this test and almost double what boys born in England or girls from the Indian sub-continent will score. This is surprising until one realizes that an Indian boy's cricket-obsessed father will probably have him practising this activity for several hours each week, thus distorting the result of this test and its reliability as a test of any innate skill. Another test is to thread three nuts onto a bolt in a timed exercise. Most boys brought up in England have some familiarity with nuts and bolts and experience little difficulty in this task. Many girls and boys from Third World countries have never seen nuts and bolts and repeatedly drop them on the floor, unable to understand why the nuts will not stick to the bolt for them in the same way that they did for the assessor when he or she was demonstrating the activity. There are a number of other similar examples.

As new tests were designed their details were published in peer-reviewed journals so as to permit the researchers to evaluate each others' findings and select the best test. Unfortunately, instead of agreeing on a common test, each country decided to use their own test, and where different tests are performed different results usually follow, leaving doubts as to the reliability and validity of the testing. The Movement ABC test is widely used in Europe, Southeast Asia and Australia, although it is not as common in the United States where the Bruininks–Oseretsky Test of Motor Proficiency is widely used. Other tests are used in other countries.

Strengths of people with dyspraxia

It is interesting that only one author, Mary Colley, has related any positive effects from dyspraxia (Colley 2006). The theory that too many brain cells are produced, that they are then allocated to tasks and that the excess cells are destroyed during a child's development (Kirby and Drew 2003, p.18) would clearly indicate that a deficiency in one area was compensated by a strength in another area. It is also likely that having to deal with a problem is likely to develop a strength. It has been suggested that those with dyspraxia are 'creative, determined, original and hard-working' possessing 'strategic-thinking and problem-solving skills' (Colley 2006) and this might be explained by the constant need to invent excuses for knocking over the furniture, to try to stop doing it again and struggling to control movements to avoid the problem if all else fails. They can also be very caring and intuitive, whilst some have become gifted writers, such as Victoria Biggs, author of the book *Caged in Chaos* (2014).

The symptoms of dyspraxia have been shown to be quite diverse and the advice of a range of specialists may be required in order to assess problems and identify potential interventions. The following table shows some of the professionals it may be appropriate to consult, some of the qualifications and expertise that should be considered when seeking assistance, the services that these specialists should be able to provide and the best times to seek their assistance.

Table 1.2: Professionals involved in evaluation of children with developmental motor concerns

Professional	Typical services provided	Qualifications	When referral is indicated
Audiologist	Perform hearing tests Obtain hearing aids or other devices	Master's degree Clinical fellowship year (CFY) National certification exam	Delayed speech or language Parent concerns about hearing Recurrent ear infections
Developmental or behavioural optometrist	Assess eye health, acuity and functional vision skills Provide interventions that may include vision therapy to address problems with visual efficiency	Completion of a four-year graduate program leading to a Doctor of Optometry (OD) Completion of postgraduate examination by one of two organizations: 1. American Academy of Optometry or 2. College of Optometrists in Vision Development	Physical signs of eyestrain Poor reading comprehension despite good vocabulary and speech Blurred or double vision Frequently losing place during reading Avoidance of visual activities
Developmental paediatrician	Diagnosis and medical management of developmental delay	Board certified paediatrician Three-year fellowship in developmental paediatrics	Suspected developmental disorder Conflict of opinion regarding diagnosis or management of developmental concerns
Geneticist	Testing to determine presence of inherited diseases	Medical degree Fellowship and board certification in genetics	Congenital malformations or stigmata Family history of mental retardation, genetic disease, chromosome abnormality, known or suspected syndrome

cont.

Professional	Typical services provided	Qualifications	When referral is indicated
Neurologist (paediatric)	Evaluation and management of nervous system disorders	Medical degree Residency in paediatric neurology Board certification	Loss or plateau of developmental skill Known or suspected seizures Unknown aetiology of developmental disability
Occupational therapist	Evaluation and management of problems performing daily living skills	**Occupational therapist:** BS or MS in occupational therapy Board certification Licensure (varies by state) Advanced paediatric certification available for paediatrics, sensory integration, or neurodevelopmental therapy **OT assistant (OTA):** AS in occupational therapy Board certification Licensure (varies by state) Must be supervised by occupational therapist	Limited ability to succeed in daily activities Limited mobility, especially fine motor Poorer nonverbal than verbal development Frustration leading to task avoidance, poor attention or problems with social interactions

Physical therapist	Evaluation and management of problems with mobility	**Physical therapist:** BS or MS in physical therapy Board certification Licensure (varies by state) Advanced paediatric certification available for paediatrics, sensory integration, or neurodevelopmental therapy **PT assistant (PTA):** AS in physical therapy Board certification Licensure (varies by state) Must be supervised by physical therapist	Delayed gross motor development or abnormal movement quality
Psychiatrist	Evaluation and management of emotional disorders	Medical degree Residency (paediatrics, internal medicine and/or psychiatry) Board certification	Suspected impairment in emotions or thought processes Serious behavioural or adjustment problems
Psychologist	Evaluation of cognitive capabilities and potential Measurement of academic achievement and educational needs Evaluation and management of problematic behaviour	**Psychologist:** Doctoral degree in psychology Internship and fellowship (varies by state) State licensure	Undiagnosed development delay Decline/regression in skill development School performance poorer than expected Inappropriate or atypical behaviour

cont.

Professional	Typical services provided	Qualifications	When referral is indicated
		School psychologist: Master's degree in psychology Supervised field experience State licensure National certification exam (NCSP)	
Social worker	Provide support to child and family around social and emotional adjustment Assist family to identify and access community services or entitlements Design and implementation of specialized programs of educational instruction	Master's degree in social work Licensure (some states) Advanced certification available (ACSW) Minimum requirements: Bachelor's degree in education One semester supervised student teaching Certifications (e.g. early childhood, reading specialist); Varies by state	Suspected child abuse or neglect Acute distress in child or family Chronic stress related to care giving responsibilities Poor parental adjustment to diagnosis Assistance needed for referral, access or funding for services Child meets eligibility requirements as defined by state for early intervention or special education
Speech language pathologist	Evaluation and management of problems with communication	Master's degree in speech/language pathology Clinical fellowship year (CFY) National certification exam Licensure (some states)	Delay or impairment in communication skills Problems with oral-motor coordination affecting speech

(Kurtz 2008)

Summary

As a society we are confining our children to smaller and smaller classrooms containing more and more technical equipment. They are required to restrain themselves to prevent themselves from damaging valuable equipment and to control their movements tightly in order to use that equipment to best effect. Previous generations have been encouraged to run wild and expend their energy and the change has not suited every child.

This move inside has, it could be argued, resulted in the identification of a new condition, dyspraxia, that is not completely understood and for which no reliable test exists. It appears to be related to other similar conditions, such as dyslexia.

Currently support for children with dyspraxia revolves around a comprehensive assessment which attempts to identify the cause and symptoms for each individual child and leads to the development of a tailored program to assist that child. This is both time consuming and expensive in my view and another way needs to be found to tackle the problem.

Chapter 2

The Causes of Dyspraxia

Despite a considerable amount of research being undertaken by scientists from a wide variety of specialisms over the last 75 years, no definitive cause of dyspraxia has yet been established.

This is not surprising when you consider that the condition has such a wide variety of symptoms that vary from child-to-child and from hour-to-hour, depending on the individual child's state of health and level of exhaustion. With no single essential symptom necessary for diagnosis, testing is problematic and, as a result, research into the condition suffers.

Samuel T. Orton, the author of the first paper on movement difficulties in children (Orton 1937), was a consultant neurologist. He claimed that the condition that he had observed was likely to be caused by lesions of the brain. A lesion is 'any structural change in an organ or tissue resulting from injury or disease' (*Collins English Dictionary*). If this claim had been confirmed it would have identified the area of the brain requiring further study, but not the full mechanism of the disorder, nor the likely interventions needed to deal with the symptoms, as lesions have several causes.

Orton compared the observed symptoms of the disorder that he identified in children with the symptoms of an adult with an acquired apraxia in later life. He felt that a unilateral brain lesion affecting the dominant hemisphere of the brain would affect the highly skilled movements and language skills that he had observed to be troubling the children. This lesion would therefore reduce the movement skills on the dominant side of the body and reduce the affected person to a state of being 'doubly left-handed' as he described it.

The state of technology in the first half of the twentieth century did not allow for brain scanners of sufficient quality to verify Dr Orton's views and the condition was presumably not considered sufficiently serious to ethically justify surgery on an experimentally significant population of those with the condition. This meant that Dr Orton's views remained unconfirmed.

Since Orton's original paper, most scientists have discounted his views on the causes of movement disorders, choosing instead to believe that the condition is caused by a deficit of neural links, but lacking the scientific evidence to support their views. A neural circuit is 'a network of nerves and their interconnections' and the brain, like your computer at home, is constantly searching for shortcuts to speed up certain movements and processes. It is not known what prompts the creation of new neural links or how they are created, but they have a vital role.

Elite athletes, who train and practise skills for several hours a day for several years, often report that their best performances occurred when their actions became automatic and they did not have to think about what they were doing as they had practised so frequently. Athletes who have achieved some of the supreme performances in sport often have no memory of the event because the neural links had become so entrenched that the action had become automatic.

The second paper on children's movement difficulties was published in 1962 (*British Medical Journal* 1962). The author reviewed the published work of three sets of researchers into groups of local children experiencing movement difficulties, from Uppsala in Sweden, from Groningen in the Netherlands and from Newcastle-upon-Tyne in England. The author attended a conference on minimal cerebral palsy in Oxford and then linked all this to his own experience and research. He observed that the Swedish children were suffering from delayed development and that they appeared to catch up given time; accepted that the Dutch children's problems had been caused by anoxia (a lack of oxygen) and poor condition at and around the time of their birth; and in the case of the English children specified that the disorder was not due to any disease or damage to the brain. After noting the similarities of the condition in the British children with those of children with lesions on the brain, he accepted this as the cause, thus supporting Samuel Orton's views on at least one cause of movement difficulties in children.

The conference attended by the author of the *British Medical Journal* article was organized by the National Spastic Society in Oxford, where consideration was given to the view that some clumsy children were afflicted with a form of minimal cerebral palsy and the author appears to have accepted that this might explain the symptoms of some children with movement difficulties.

The view that dyspraxia is a form of borderline or minimal cerebral palsy has been widely accepted by several subsequent authors (Hadders-Algra 2003) without any further research or comment. With both conditions sharing the same characteristic symptoms of abnormal muscle tone, reflexes, motor development and coordination, it is easy to understand this view. It is particularly interesting that the incidence of cerebral palsy has been strongly linked to anoxia at or about the time of birth or during pregnancy. Two of the four sources referred to in the *British Medical Journal* article had suggested anoxia as a factor in the incidence of dyspraxia albeit one doing so indirectly.

It is now almost 50 years since the publication of the second research paper into children's movement skills. The two papers published between 1937 and 1962 identified a number of issues which appeared to the authors to be significant in the incidence of the observed movement difficulties in children:

- lesions on the brain

- a lack of neural links

- delayed development, from which children recover given time

- minimal cerebral palsy

- anoxia

- disorder not due to any disease or damage to the brain.

Recent research, using some of the latest technology, has confirmed most of these issues (Geuze 2007). Dyspraxia is not due to any disease or damage to the brain. Scanners are now able to identify the lesions on the brain which have been linked to the incidence of dyspraxia. Specialists still suspect that dyspraxia is linked to a lack of neural links, although there is currently no way of confirming their presence or absence or how they are formed. Dyspraxia is still seen as a developmental condition affecting movement skills in children, although it is recognized that the symptoms persist into adolescence and even adulthood unless suitable training to improve skills or coping strategies is developed. Anoxia, the lack of oxygen at or around the time of birth, with its links to dyspraxia and cerebral palsy is still seen as significant.

Support for the view that difficulties during pregnancy, particularly at or around the time of birth and quite possibly linked with anoxia, may be associated with movement disorders in children, came in 1992 when three scientists published research, although no reason for them forming similar opinions at the same time has been identified. Birth trauma could cause the baby to be deprived of oxygen and therefore support the earlier research or it may be that the trauma is a symptom of the condition rather than a cause of it and further research is clearly required. Another researcher suggested that a large number of minor abnormalities, such as immature brain cells or congenital tumours, occurred during pre-natal development and that the body compensates for these problems by re-wiring around them and that this unique re-wiring may cause the difficulties experienced in movement skills (Farnham-Diggory 1992). Other research suggested that some children may have retained some primitive reflexes that cause shrugging, twitching, fidgeting and many of the symptoms of dyspraxia (Blythe 1992). This could have the effect of sending a signal intended for one limb to all four limbs so that they receive four times their anticipated number of messages, become confused and make mistakes. On occasion, not realizing that they have received an incorrect message, the limbs start to react before cancelling the movement, giving the impression of fidgeting.

Other factors linked by research to the incidence of dyspraxia include birth trauma, such as premature birth, precipitate birth, late delivery, forceps delivery, caesarean section, breech delivery, foetal anoxia and induced labour and mothers lacking essential omega oils during pregnancy.

Symptoms similar to those of dyspraxia have been identified in children whose mothers have consumed alcohol during pregnancy even in relatively insignificant amounts. This has been called Foetal Alcohol Syndrome, and there are a number of symptoms (McCreight 1997) but they are relatively minor and may appear insignificant when any movement difficulties are identified during an assessment of the child away from the presence of the mother many years after the children are born. Almost all social and recreational drugs are capable of crossing the placenta and causing death and congenital deformation of the baby (Pollard 2007). Little evidence exists as to whether these drugs can cause movement disorders, as research has focused on the higher-end problems of causing death and congenital deformation rather than movement difficulties. The strength and nature of these substances suggests that there could be some connection, but this remains to be tested by scientific research.

The lack of a precise cause for dyspraxia has led to the American Psychiatric Association specifying unusually in their diagnostic criteria for the condition that 'the coordination difficulties are not due to a general medical condition' (American Psychiatric Association 2000). The full definition of dyspraxia in the manual is included in Chapter 1.

In the absence of a clear definition for dyspraxia, it is essential to have the best possible understanding of the causes of the disorder. Only in this way will it be possible to postulate the possibilities for preventing the disorder and the ways in which children with movement difficulties can best be helped. As the majority of books on the subject of dyspraxia have been written by educationalists and medical therapists, or are of the self-help variety, their authors are not qualified to comment on the causes of a condition which is generally accepted to be of a neurological nature and they have refrained from doing so.

Related research into the causes of dyslexia

Research into dyspraxia has failed to identify factors relating to the incidence of the condition and little other than speculation exists that may assist future research. In such circumstances the best solution may be a sideways glance at similar areas of study. Dyslexia is a specific learning disorder, like dyspraxia, and a great deal of research has been undertaken into the causes of the condition.

Whereas dyspraxia is often perceived as an 'inconvenience' in that children with the condition are a nuisance and knock over the furniture and disturb the classroom, dyslexia is a serious problem. Children who are unable to read have little place in the educational system, are unlikely to graduate or to take up employment that reflects their intellect, education, ability or ambition. Teachers look bad; success rates are lowered; questions are asked; something needs to be done. The serious nature of the condition is reflected in the amount of research that has been undertaken into it.

Children when reading require good skills to identify the characters and sound out the words that they see written on the page, but they also need the magnocellular area of the brain (see below) to be working efficiently to see what is written on the page. Those children with dyslexia appear to experience difficulties in the *magnocellular* part of the brain which measures time, distance and motion. It identifies and measures movements, including those of the head, which it is then able to balance out so that it effectively stabilizes images viewed by the child (Stein 2003). In dyslexic children that stability is lacking and the child's brain sees a blurred image on a page and in some cases may even see the words moving about on the page. These effects, separately and combined, make it very difficult for the child to read. It is very easy to understand how difficulties in the part of the brain that measures time, distance and motion could affect movement skills and cause children to suffer from dyspraxia. When the brains of those with dyslexia were compared with control brains, it was found that the magnocells in the dyslexic brains were 30 per cent smaller and significantly more disorganized than in the control brains. Consistent with this researchers recorded reduced and delayed averaged evoked potentials in response to a visual motion stimulus in alive dyslexics (Lehmkuhle and

Williams 1993; Livingstone *et al.* 1991) although the results have been disputed (Victor *et al.* 1993).

Children with dyslexia also experience difficulties with their phonological skills that allow them to understand the sounds that certain letters and combinations of letters make. Phonological skills have no apparent effect on movement skills and will be passed over quickly here, but the fact that dyslexia is caused by a combination of two factors may assist in explaining the causes of dyspraxia and the reasons why it has proved so difficult to understand. The magnocellular system may be a factor in the incidence of dyspraxia but if it were the only factor then every child with dyslexia would also have dyspraxia. Phonological skills do not relate to movement skills and if they related to dyspraxia then similarly every child with dyslexia would also have dyspraxia. It would therefore be reasonable to assume that there is a second factor in the incidence of dyspraxia, but that it has not yet been identified. The fact that there are two factors and that both were required to be present for dyspraxia to occur would go some way to explain the difficulties that have been experienced in identifying the cause of dyspraxia.

There is a theory in neurodevelopmental science that during their normal development children produce more brain cells than they need. Later, as the child develops, between 15 and 85 per cent of the brain cells produced are destroyed by the body in a remodelling and rationalization process. The neuronal links between these brain cells will be lost at the same time as the cells themselves are destroyed. The theory proposes that although the final number of brain cells conforms to certain rules and varies little from child to child, the size of each functional area of the brain may vary at this time from child to child (Kirby and Drew 2003, p.18). This apparently random process could clearly result in affected children being advantaged and disadvantaged in various abilities and functions and may explain a lack of magnocellular cells in certain children.

Summary

Research into the causes of dyspraxia remains at a very early stage. It has shown a link between the incidence of lesions in the brain and the incidence of dyspraxia and there is speculation that anoxia in pregnancy particularly at or around the time of birth and trauma at birth may be a factor – but there is little reliable research to support any of this. The similarities between dyslexia and dyspraxia appear to provide the strongest basis for finding a cause for the disorder, with a lack of fatty acids during pregnancy, and a reduction in the size and number of magnocellular cells requiring further investigation. None of this, however, suggests a viable intervention that could reduce the incidence or symptoms of the condition, other than fatty acid supplementation. It thus appears likely that the best intervention may have to come from methods designed to improve skills in the general population.

Recent technological advances have permitted the development of scanners capable of examining the human brain in sufficient detail to show lesions (structural changes in an organ or tissue resulting from injury or disease) on the brain that have been associated with the incidence of movement difficulties in children (Geuze 2007), but the exact mechanism of how these lesions result in the symptoms of dyspraxia has not been explained.

Chapter 3

Further Research Since the First Edition

Beating Dyspraxia with a Hop, Skip and a Jump was the first book written by this author. Confronted by that most frightening of images, a blank sheet of paper and with an intention to satisfy all the reader's questions, it quickly became clear that there were a considerable number of questions that would go unanswered.

Dyspraxia is a bit of a black hole at present. The six years of research that had gone into a PhD had allowed the author to read every other book on the subject and had satisfied him that he was up-to-date with the latest research and that it was not a matter of ignorance, but rather a matter that the knowledge did not currently exist.

Writing a book exposes an author. Will anybody read it? What feedback will there be? In the three years since the first edition of *Beating Dyspraxia* there have been half a dozen published reviews of the book; five of these reviews have been positive and one has been indifferent. Several parents of sufferers have contacted the author with specific questions about the condition of dyspraxia and its effects on sufferers.

This correspondence reflects the concerns of those affected by the condition, but it also highlights that there are further areas to be investigated and further answers to be obtained.

What is known

The author undertook the research on which this book is based at the University of Edinburgh and, in the three years since the publication of the first edition, has read a great deal about the work of Professor Peter Higgs, the man who theorised the existence of the Higgs Bosun in 1964. Professor Higgs could not see or hear or feel the particle that he knew existed but from the reaction of the other particles that he could see and hear and feel, he knew that there had to be something else out there.

Put simply, he described it to be like Margaret Thatcher entering a room. She was a relatively short woman and as such if you were standing across the room, you would not see her enter. However, her effect on other people in the room was such that there was an increase of volume caused by people announcing her arrival to friends and there was a surge forward as people struggled to get closer to her, so that at the back of the crowd you could feel the movement. The independent observer at the back of the room had not seen, heard or felt Margaret Thatcher, but he just *knew* that she had entered the room because of her effect on those at the front of the room.

It was only in 2012, almost half a century after Professor Higgs went public with his beliefs that scientists at the CERN Laboratory in Switzerland were able to confirm the existence of his particle, so that Professor Higgs was awarded a Nobel Prize.

There is a consensus among teachers, who work with young children on a daily basis, that there has been a drop off in the movement skills of young children over the last 100 years, but they have no idea what has caused it or how to test for it. Doctors who have been consulted about the problem have confirmed that they agree that a problem exists, but because nobody felt the need to conduct research on children's movement skills until the problem existed and had no way of measuring the problem until they looked into the matter, there are no data to confirm this belief.

In fact, we have a very successful intervention that can bring about an 87 per cent reduction in symptoms, without being able to define the condition or recognizing it.

Definition of the condition

The word dyspraxia comes from the Greek, 'dys' meaning poor or difficult and 'praxia' meaning movement or movement planning. This would mean that the problem existed in the brain of the sufferer, where all planning takes place. However, if this were true, how is it that a strength training program reduces the symptoms of the condition?

There is clear evidence that strength training improves the appearance and function of muscles. It is only necessary to look at a bodybuilding book in a newsagents to know that strength training increases the size, shape and tone of muscles. A glance inside a gym will also confirm that trained muscles lift more weight and are therefore more efficient than untrained muscles. Scientific research has confirmed that trained muscles also improve the control of the movement of these muscles.

It has long become accepted by scientists that at the ends of muscles, where tendons link them to bones, there are sensors which feed back data to the brain on the tensions affecting the muscle, so that the brain will understand when weights that are being lifted are becoming dangerously heavy so that the brain can decide to stop attempting to lift them before they cause damage and injury to the body. Perhaps these sensors do a little more than that and contribute to other decisions made in the brain, but which affect movement across the body? This is clearly beyond the knowledge and skills of a sports coach, but perhaps worthy of further research?

Dyspraxia also has a number of other names, one of which is developmental coordination disorder (DCD). This name tells us a great deal about the condition and its causes. It is a developmental condition; that is, children are born with it and it improves as they grow older and mature, without any other intervention. The name also tells us that the condition is focused on the coordination of movement.

From the research that has already been undertaken we know that the condition is strongly linked to muscular weakness in children and that when the muscular weakness has been removed, at least in part, 72 per cent of the other symptoms of the condition also disappear. It may be that eight weeks of strength training is not enough to completely eliminate the weakness and that perhaps another 8 or 16 weeks' training is required and that when this has been completed there will be a 100 per cent reduction in the symptoms of the dyspraxia.

Symptoms of the condition

The only thing that we know about dyspraxia is that it adversely affects movement skills in children. The strong correlation between the incidence of dyspraxia and muscular weakness and the effectiveness of strength training in improving the movement skills may now allow the muscular weakness to be accepted as a symptom of dyspraxia.

Causes of the condition

Dyspraxia occurs during gestation and many scientists have claimed to have discovered the first signs of the condition up to six weeks before the birth of the child. Possible causes cited have included a lack of omega oils, lesions on the brain and a lack of neural links in the brain. Clearly, further research is required here.

Test for the condition

As has been previously discussed, there are a wide range of ways of testing children's movement skills and dozens of tests have been designed to do this. In the US the Bruininks-Oseretsky test has been adopted and in the UK there is the Movement ABC test, which has now been updated to the Movement ABC 2. These tests require a considerable amount of equipment and a great deal of time to complete them and they produce a result which is comparative rather than absolute and which does not take into account the child's health or state of exhaustion.

Cure for the condition

Research has shown that an eight-week strength training intervention will bring about a 72 per cent reduction in the symptoms of the condition. Research has also shown that a praxis improving intervention will increase the reduction in symptoms from 72 per cent to 87 per cent. Clearly, it is possible that increasing the length of the strength training intervention to 16 or 24 weeks may increase the effectiveness of the intervention.

When something relieves one or more of the symptoms it is called an intervention. It cannot be described as a cure until doctors are able to understand how and why it works. Clearly, there is more work to be done to understand why strength training reduces the symptoms of dyspraxia.

So why is more research not being undertaken?

Research is complex and expensive and funding is generally directed, quite properly, towards life threatening conditions, which dyspraxia is not. Dyspraxia used to be known as clumsy child syndrome and was seen as a few children knocking over the furniture.

Dyspraxia is only recognized in North America, Western Europe, Australia and New Zealand. This is because in these places classrooms are small and space is limited, and clumsy children knock over the furniture and cause problems for the teacher. I recently returned to the school that I attended half a century ago. I saw that the buildings were almost unchanged, but that now there were large plasma televisions, personal computers and laptops. This meant that any child lacking good movement skills caused some very expensive damage. In Asia and Africa, where space is more readily available, it is possible to make larger classrooms where more space is available and clumsy children are less of a problem.

Part II

The Exercise Programs

Chapter 4

The Importance of Exercise

But we do know what the Greeks knew: that intelligence and skill can only function at the peak of their capacity when the body is healthy and strong; that hardy spirits and tough minds usually inhabit sound bodies.

(President Kennedy 1960)

That which is used develops, and that which is not used wastes away.

(Hippocrates, fourth century BC)

Growth, maturation and development

From conception to the age of 19, children spend almost 20 years growing, maturing and developing. From an embryo a young man may grow to close to 2 metres tall and 100 kg in bodyweight. His fitness will improve proportionately. From being unable even to roll away from a potential predator, he will be able to sprint 100 metres in as little as 10 seconds. This process of growth, maturation and development (and eventually degeneration) follows a pre-determined plan from conception to death.

Whilst each of us is an individual, affected by both nature and nurture, our development follows strict guidelines, so that doctors and physiologists are able to produce tables showing patterns of development, which can be used by health visitors, school nurses and parents concerned at a child's rate of development. Specialists can assess our children's growth, maturation and development and identify any problems at the first opportunity so that these may be investigated, diagnosed and, if necessary, treated, as quickly as possible. The areas covered in these tables may include:

- growth, such as height, weight, seated height, limb length and size of head

- physiological development, such as strength, endurance, fitness, speed, etc.

- development in movement skills and the ages at which these skills are achieved

- landmarks in speech and language skills

- cognitive and perceptual development

- perceptual and social skills.

Table 3.1 is an example of such a presentation of typical development.

Table 3.1

Age	Fine motor	Gross motor	Speech language	Cognitive/perceptual	Perceptual/social
3 months	Hands remain open during rest	Head lags behind when pulled to sitting from lying on back	Coos/smiles in response to pleasant tones Laughs aloud Searches for sound with eyes	When lying on back, promptly looks at toy and follows with eyes	Shows anticipation of bottle/food through facial response
6 months	Passes toy from hand to hand when lying on back Rakes at tiny object using all fingers	Plays with feet while lying on back Rolls in both directions Sits with hands propped forward Stands and bounces when held by both hands	Pays attention to music or singing Understands 'hi' and 'bye-bye' Imitates familiar sounds, babbles (e.g. 'wawa', 'baba')	Shakes rattle on purpose	Holds own bottle Drinks from cup that is held by adult Mouths/gums hard cookie or cracker
9 months	Grasps block with fingers, not palm of hand Wrist is extended (bent back) during grasp of block	Head leads when pulled to sitting from lying on back Creeps or crawls on all fours Sits independently with hands free for play Pulls to stand at low table	Stops activity when name is called Understands 'no' Uses some gesture language Participates in 'pat-a-cake,' 'peek-a-boo'	Holds one block or toy in each hand and bangs together at midline	Feeds self cracker Finger feeds small bits of food (like cereal or cut-up vegetables)

cont.

Age	Fine motor	Gross motor	Speech language	Cognitive/perceptual	Perceptual/social
12 months	Builds tower of two blocks Uses mature pinch grasp (thumb and tip of forefinger) Holds crayon using fisted grasp Helps to turn pages in a book	Stands alone without support Takes first steps	Responds to simple commands without any gestures Knows one body part Beginning to use single words meaningfully	Imitates scribbling with crayon	Brings pre-filled spoon to mouth, but spills Holds handle of cup while drinking Holds out arms and legs for dressing
15 months	Builds tower of three blocks Can place small pegs in pegboard	Crawling is discarded except on stairs Plays while squatting Gets to standing position without holding on to anything	Points to object when named Points to several body parts	Fills container with blocks Scribbles with crayon without demonstration	Shows awareness/discomfort when diaper is soiled Scoops food with spoon (spills)
18 months	Builds tower of four blocks Turns pages of book, two or three at a time	Seats self in small chair Climbs stairs holding rail	Refers to self by name Puts together two-word sentences	Inserts simple shapes into a formboard	Removes socks Sometimes indicates the need to eliminate before an accident Chews semi-solid food

24 months	Builds tower of seven blocks Strings small beads	Kicks a ball forward Jumps with both feet leaving floor	Produces 25–200 words Jargon has disappeared Points to pictures in book Enjoys listening to simple stories and nursery rhymes	Matches three colours Imitates strokes (circular scribble, straight vertical line) with crayon	Holds glass with two hands Has bladder control Imitates housework Drinks from straw Recognizes edible/nonedible food Helps pull down pants Finds armholes to pullover shirt
30 months	Builds tower of nine blocks Turns pages of book one at a time Shows preference for one hand	Climbs stairs with one foot to each step Stands on one foot briefly Rides tricycle	Understands taking turns	Imitates circle, horizontal stroke with crayon Names own drawings, even if unrecognizable	Uses napkin Unfastens large buttons Puts away jacket/toys Assists in pulling on socks
36 months	Builds tower of ten blocks Holds crayon with fingers like adult Cuts 'fringe' with scissors	Runs on toes Runs, turning sharp corners without falling Performs broad jump about 12 inches' distance	Vocabulary of about 1000 words Carries on purposeful conversation No longer repeats or echoes others	Imitates cross with crayon Names and sorts objects by colour Counts three objects correctly	Feeds self with fork, spoon, rarely spilling Zips and unzips zipper once engaged Snaps front snaps Buttons large buttons Puts on shoes, wrong foot Turns water on/off

cont.

Age	Fine motor	Gross motor	Speech language	Cognitive/perceptual	Perceptual/social
42 months	Can place ten pellets or raisins in small bottle within 25 seconds Shifts crayon up/down in fingers to adjust	Stands on tiptoe for ten seconds Hops on one foot		Names some letters and numbers	Puts shoes on correct feet Knows front from back of clothing Puts on mittens Can undo buckle Blows nose into tissue
4 years	Can place ten pellets or raisins in small bottle within 20 seconds Cuts 1-inch [2.5cm] wide line within half inch	Performs somersault Catches a beanbag with the hands (not against body) Performs broad jump about 24 inches [60cm] distance	Can recall four digits in sequence Speech is 90 per cent understandable	Copies square with crayon Draws one or two letters, numbers	Removes pullover garment Puts socks on correctly Washes/dries face/hands effectively Runs brush/comb through hair Places dirty clothes in hamper Sets table with help
5 years	Can place ten pellets or raisins in small bottle within 10 seconds Cuts out square within quarter inch	Runs through obstacle course avoiding obstacles Skips with alternating swing Stands on one foot for 10 seconds		Counts ten objects correctly Prints first name Draws recognizable face with eyes, nose, mouth	Drinks from water fountain without help Serves self and carries tray in line Wipes self after toileting Dresses without supervision Ties the half knot on shoes Looks both ways to cross street Bathes/showers when reminded

Age	Fine motor	Gross motor	Language/play	Academic	Self-help
6 years	Can move coin from palm of hand to fingers to place in soda machine	Performs one each of sit-up and knee push-up; Rides two-wheeler	Likes silly stories and riddles	Copies triangle and crude diamond; Prints all letters and numbers one to nine without a model to copy; Prints last name; Performs simple addition and subtraction; Discriminates left from right	Uses knife/fork to eat; Ties bow; Closes fastener on back of clothes; Cares for nose effectively; Initiates phone calls to others; Fastens back buttons; Adjusts faucet temperature for bath
7 years			Reading and writing at school	Prints three to four word sentences; Reversals in writing are no longer common	Styles hair; Knows value of coins
8 years					Bathes/showers independently; Remembers to wash ears; Sweeps, mops or vacuums floors
10 years				Writes in cursive instead of printing	Ties necktie; Uses stove or microwave independently; Uses household cleaning agents appropriately; Uses deodorant
12 years					Counts change for purchases costing more than $1 [~65p]

(Kurtz 2008, pp.18–22)

Factors in development

Development is directed by genetics. It has often been said that the most important decision that a child wanting to become an Olympic champion has to make is choosing his or her parents. By the time that the child has been born, many genetic factors have been fixed, although researchers investigating the human genome hope to be able to make changes to it in the near future. There are, however, a range of lifestyle factors that do influence growth, maturation and development. These include nutrition and exercise as well as ensuring adequate rest and relaxation, abstinence from cigarettes and alcohol and a secure home environment where excessive stress is avoided. This book will focus on three of the most important and most easily improved factors. It will comment briefly on nutrition and sleep, concentrate on exercise, and pass over the social issues.

Nutrition

Until the past 50 years, finding food of sufficient quality and quantity has been a problem throughout history for most people in the world. Only after the restrictions imposed by the Second World War were relaxed did improved transport links provide the food that most people needed. As soon as food was easily available at reasonable prices, industry began investigating processing technologies in order to make food more attractive but which increased sugar and salt levels and led to obesity. Obesity should not be a problem for young children who are supplied with an ideal, nutritionally balanced diet that will ensure for them a long and healthy life and who are restrained from obtaining significant amounts of unsuitable, unhealthy food. Government programs are providing the training on nutrition that should prevent adults or children from being able to claim that they lack the knowledge to make informed decisions on what they eat.

Sleep

Growing children require approximately eight hours of sleep each night. There is an old saying that states that an hour of sleep before midnight is worth two after midnight and this certainly has an element of truth to it. Modern lifestyles tend to divert children from these guidelines. Many children have televisions, DVD players, computers and computer gaming machines in their bedrooms. These machines encourage children to stay up late and entertain them if they wake up during the night, so that instead of turning over and going back to sleep they stay awake and play. Many children take mobile telephones to bed with them and are then awoken by other children calling or texting them. All these machines are best left downstairs at night so that children can sleep undisturbed.

Exercise

There is now an almost universal acceptance that exercise is an essential factor in a healthy lifestyle. In adults, frequent and regular aerobic exercise has been shown to help prevent or treat serious, life-threatening conditions such as high blood pressure, heart disease, obesity, Type 2 diabetes, insomnia and depression (US Department of Health and Human Services 1999). Frequent and regular strength exercise contributes positively to improving muscle strength and joint mobility, maintaining a healthy bodyweight and building and maintaining healthy bone density (Baechle and Earle 2008). According to the World Health Organization (WHO), a lack of physical activity contributes to approximately 17 per cent of heart disease and diabetes, 12 per cent of falls in the elderly, and 10 per cent of breast cancer and colon cancer. In fact, exercise increases our physical fitness and, as part of a balanced exercise program, each of the sub-components of physical fitness including:

- strength

- endurance

- muscular endurance

- flexibility

- speed

- body composition.

There is also evidence that vigorous exercise (90–95% of VO2 Max [the amount of oxygen consumed during maximum exertion]) is more beneficial than moderate exercise (40–70% of VO2 Max). Some studies (Wislett, Ellingsen and Kemi 2009) have shown that vigorous exercise executed by healthy individuals can increase endorphins, and increase testosterone and growth hormone, effects that are not as fully realized with moderate exercise.

Not everyone benefits equally from exercise. There is tremendous variation in individual response to training: where most people will see a moderate increase in endurance from aerobic exercise, some individuals will as much as double their oxygen uptake, while others can never augment endurance (Bouchard *et al.* 1999). Similarly, only a minority of people will show significant muscle growth after prolonged weight training, while a larger fraction experience improvements in strength. This genetic variation in improvement from training is one of the key physiological differences between elite athletes and the larger population (Kolata 2002).

In children the physiological response to exercise is different from that in adults. For children, exercise is a developmental activity, essential to their physical, physiological, psychological, social and emotional growth. Playing increases their strength and fitness, encourages their hearts and lungs to develop and allows them to build self-image and self-confidence, learn to mix with their peers and deal with success and failure.

Children are generally healthy and do not as a rule suffer from the conditions resulting from a lack of exercise in adults, such as high blood pressure, heart disease, Type 2 diabetes, insomnia and depression, until much later in life, although we are starting to see a problem with children suffering from obesity. Whilst there is currently little scientific evidence that a lack of exercise immediately affects the health and fitness of our young people (Rowland 2007), it does, of course, build patterns of living that have been shown to cause the health problems associated with inactivity in later life. A lack of exercise in childhood may eventually prove to cause the problems that occur in later life, making them worse than they would otherwise have been, but further long-term research will be required to confirm this.

Exercise in the past

Since the start of the Industrial Revolution in the late eighteenth century there have been doubts raised about the health and fitness of the younger generation. The movement away from an agricultural economy to an urban industrial economy reduced the reliance on manual labour by increasing the use of alternative forms of energy such as coal, steam and water, causing fundamental changes to a range of socio-economic and cultural factors and eventually to the lifestyles of all working people.

A number of authors have felt the need to go into print on this subject with two of those being worthy of special mention. First, Max Nordau published a book entitled *Degeneration* in 1892 and introduced his concept of 'fin de siècle', which he described as 'the dusk of the nations' and the 'autumn of human life' (Nordau 1892, pp.1–2) whereby degeneration would lead to the eventual decline and fall of the human race, explaining that the Industrial Revolution had led to large towns – more railways – more alcohol consumption – more food – less exercise, and – degeneration. The book was so successful that it had to be reprinted six times in the first year and is still in print today.

In 1899 Lieutenant-Colonel Robert Baden-Powell published a book entitled *Aids to Scouting* aimed at soldiers (Baden-Powell 1899). The next year he returned home, promoted to Major General and a popular hero after his success in defending the city during the Siege of Mafeking in the course of the Boer War. When he heard that the Director General of the War Office had issued a memorandum pointing out that between 40 and 60 per cent of those applying to enlist in the army were unfit for service, he was prompted to revise his book so that it addressed teenage boys and highlighted the need for outdoor physical activities, re-publish it as *Scouting for Boys* (Baden-Powell 1908) and set up the International Scouting Movement, as Europe prepared for the First World War.

After the Second World War the restrictions that had been imposed on urban children in order to ensure their safety during the Blitz, and which had prevented them from playing in the streets, were lifted and they swiftly returned to spending their days running, jumping, playing football and climbing trees. From the 1950s onwards greater affluence, mass car ownership and modern housing estates combined with an increased perception of danger from paedophiles following a number of widely publicized cases persuaded parents that children could best be protected within the home, entertained by their new electronic toys of television and radio and later by videos, video games and computers and their successors.

Physical education

PE at school is generally failing to provide the exercise and hard work that our children need. Teachers of PE are being restrained in the way that they deal with their students, for fear of provoking allegations of bullying. Requests for toilet and drinks breaks cannot be delayed however frequent and frivolous and requests for treatment of injuries cannot be denied however trivial the claimed injury. Few primary schools employ qualified PE teachers and, as a result, those teaching PE restrict themselves to simple games and activities, which the children find unchallenging and do not enjoy. This causes the children to seek opportunities to escape from the lessons, by producing letters from parents exempting them from participation, by requesting toilet or drink breaks or by seeking attention for minor injuries, all of which their managers require the teachers to respond to positively. One school visited recently, a Sports College with responsibility for the local sports partnership, recorded just 11 per cent participation in PE classes during the year in question. In comparison with physical education lessons, children sent out to play unsupervised are naturally competitive and derive great pleasure from competing against their peers in any game or activity. No child ever sought permission to miss play through an injury. The children become deeply involved in these games and activities and honestly lose all track of time. These children will last for exceptional periods of time without a drink break or a toilet break and with no adults handing out sympathy, see no point in reporting injuries and therefore carry on playing regardless.

Exercise and children with dyspraxia

Children between the ages of five and eight years develop their own perception of themselves and their place in society. They form views on their appearance, intelligence and abilities.

Those who are unable to control their movements in class and who have become the butt of jokes for their 'clumsiness' and who are unable to impress with their skills in playground games will suffer in terms of self-esteem. They will seek ways of avoiding embarrassment, and these strategies usually include avoiding sport and games (Macintyre 2002), often claiming that they are 'too rough, boring or too tiring' (Geuze 2007, p.14).

Exercise is more important for those with dyspraxia. Several researchers have argued that *an active lifestyle is even more important for those who have disabilities* or disorders than for the general population (Cooper *et al.* 1999; Steele *et al.* 1996; van der Ploeg *et al.* 2004). Their argument is based on the beneficial effects of exercise on the functional abilities of persons with disabilities or disorders. They also suggest that exercise reduces the risk of secondary conditions that are physical, medical, cognitive or emotional, or psycho-social consequences, and which a person with a primary disabling condition is predisposed to experience (Simeonsson, McMillen and Huntington 2002).

Child fitness levels

Exercise improves fitness and in order to understand why exercise has an important effect on dyspraxia it is necessary to look at children's fitness. Child fitness levels are the focus of a great deal of government attention, with almost daily reports in the national press relating to the latest scientific research and updates in government policy. Childhood obesity is recognized by the WHO as one of the top ten problems facing us as we enter the twenty-first century (WHO 1992). Cardiovascular fitness levels among ten-year-old children are dropping at the rate of 4.8 per cent per decade (Sandercock *et al.* 2010). Sports coaches and PE teachers complain about the lack of movement skills of our children. Government advisors argue about which of these aspects of fitness should be given priority in their attempts to improve the health of the nation (BBC 2009). The health and wellbeing of our children is the cause of almost universal concern.

Obesity has benefited from considerable research (Berkey *et al.* 2000; Booth *et al.* 2001; Smith and Biddle 2008) and substantial efforts have been made to reduce the fatness of school-age children by taking statutory powers to close fast food restaurants near schools (*The Independent* 2009), by attempting to control school-time meals for their nutritional content and by improving labelling of the content of food supplied in restaurants and stores (FSA 2009). Governments are attempting to increase statutory provision of physical education for all children in an attempt to improve their fitness. Children's movement skills and the ways to improve them are now the subject of advanced study. Regrettably, little is being done to improve the children's movement skills, possibly due to a lack of knowledge and a focus on children's health, nutrition and diet in regular PE classes.

Strength

Strength has long been recognized as a factor in the incidence of dyspraxia (Platt 2010; Raynor 1989; Raynor 2001). Children who are weaker than their peers at school are more likely to have dyspraxia and the symptoms are likely to improve if they undertake strength training (Platt 2010; Raynor 1989; Raynor 2001). Strength is defined as 'the ability to generate maximum external force' (Zatsiorsky and Kraemer 2006, p.21).

With a definition discussing maximum external force and images of weightlifters breaking world records for the clean and jerk by holding 263 kg/580 lbs overhead and powerlifters breaking the world record for the squat with 457.5 kg/1008.6 lbs, it can be little surprise that strength is commonly associated with men with freakish muscles lifting outrageous weights. However, strength is clearly a measurable variable and whilst the champions are breaking their records some people lack the strength necessary to remain healthy and to perform the tasks of daily life. The National Strength and Conditioning Association (NSCA) of the USA has produced its *Basic Guidelines for the Resistance Training of Athletes* (Pearson *et al.* 2000), and the British Association of Sports and Exercise Sciences (BASES) its *Guidelines for Resistance Exercise in Young People* (Stratton *et al.* 2004). The two documents express similar views with the latter describing strength as 'essential for healthy living and the development of the healthy child' (pp.383–390).

It has long been recognized that one of the most frequent causes of injury is muscle imbalance (Chandler *et al.* 1992; Croisier *et al.* 2002; Heiser *et al.* 1984), which is usually caused by a lack of strength in a muscle. This can occur at any age, with some children emerging from the womb with muscle imbalances caused by awkward body positions whilst in the womb, and with some older people degenerating and losing muscle strength unequally around the body. Treatment for all such injuries must include the strengthening of the muscle to eliminate the weakness that caused the injury or it will be likely to recur. This treatment will follow the same principles as all strength training whether designed to build weightlifting champions or to assist recovery following injury.

Everybody needs enough strength to live their life. A woman in her 80s requires the strength to perform a half squat with her bodyweight or she will be unable to rise from her armchair to make herself a cup of tea or to prepare a meal and if she is unable to do that she will be unable to live without support and assistance. The exercise program suggested by her physiotherapist will probably not involve tracksuits, leotards or metal weights but instead stress the need to keep getting out of the chair in order to strengthen the muscles of the legs and hips.

Physiotherapists are required to assist a substantial number of people with general or specific muscular weaknesses and most hospital physiotherapy departments contain multigyms, dynamometers (instruments designed to measure the force exerted by a muscle), medicine balls and sometimes even weight training bars, weights and dumbbells in order to assist them in this task.

Table 3.2: Physiological adaptations to resistance training	
Variable	Resistance training adaptations
Performance	
Muscular strength	Increases
Muscular endurance	Increases for high power output
Aerobic power	No change or increases slightly
Maximal rate of force production	Increases
Vertical jump	Ability increases
Anacrobic powcr	Increases
Sprint speed	Improves
Metabolic energy stores	
Stored ATP	
Stored creatine phosphate	Increases
Stored glycogen	Increases
Stored triglycerides	Increases
	May increase
Connective tissue	
Ligament strength	May increase
Tendon strength	May increase
Collagen content	May increase
Bone density	No change or increases
Body composition	
% body fat	Decreases
Fat-free mass	Increases

(Reprinted, with permission, from N.A. Ratamess 2008, p.96. 'Adaptations to anaerobic training programs.' In Essentials of Strength Training and Conditioning, 3rd ed., edited for the National Strength and Conditioning Association by T.R. Baechle and R.W. Earle (Champaign, IL: Human Kinetics), 96.)

Children with dyspraxia have been shown to have slack muscles and to lack muscle tone. They have been described as lacking in strength in their fingers, hands and wrists (Oliveira *et al.* 2006), which may relate to the difficulties that have been identified in completing a number of fine motor skills such as writing and drawing. Table 3.2 lists the physiological adaptations to resistance training and when these are compared with the symptoms of dyspraxia (see pages 20–22) it can be seen that these adaptations will benefit those children with dyspraxia.

Recent research of mine assessed the strength of approximately 500 primary school children and compared it with the results of tests of fine and gross motor skills contained in the Movement ABC test used to identify cases of dyspraxia (Platt 2010). The results showed a clear and significant correlation between the children lacking in strength and those with movement difficulties. When the same children had completed a six-week strength training program the tests were repeated and their results in the tests of fine and gross motor skills showed a clear and significant improvement.

These results confirm the work of Australian physiologist Annette Raynor (Raynor 1989; Raynor 2001) who revealed a link between dyspraxia and difficulties in muscle activation and co-activation (explained in Chapter 4). When these were improved through a strength training program, they combined to lead to improved neural control of movement. The results also confirm the results of the two superintendent physiotherapists, Lee and Smith (1998), mentioned in the first chapter, who found that an eight-week strength training program, based on individualized observations of children with dyspraxia, produced a 72 per cent reduction in their symptoms. However, Lee and Smith's program was found to be too expensive to implement due to the time commitment required by specialist paediatric physiotherapists.

Movement planning and universal movement skills

As previously discussed, dyspraxia, comes from the Greek words, 'dys', meaning poor or difficult, and 'praxis', meaning movement or movement planning. Dyspraxia is a developmental disorder in which children experience difficulties in controlling their movements, usually due to poor movement planning.

A number of very complex calculations have to be completed before any movement can take place. If I am watching the television and decide that I am thirsty, I must then decide what I am going to do about being thirsty. What do I want to drink? What is available? Where is it? Then I must decide what I need to do to get it.

My first real challenge is getting myself out of the armchair. I need to stand up. This requires me to move my centre of gravity over my feet, keeping myself constantly in balance so that I do not fall over. I must then straighten my legs so that I am standing upright. Now I need to walk to the kitchen and I need to work out a route, preferably one that is free from books, papers or obstructions so that I do not slip over.

When I get to the kitchen I may need to stretch up to take hold of a clean cup from the shelf, take a grip on the cup that is not strong enough to break it yet strong enough that I will not drop it. I may then need to bend down to remove a carton of milk from the fridge. Throughout the stretching and bending process I need to maintain my centre of gravity over my base, formed by the area between my feet, so that I do not fall over.

There then follow some fine manual skills as I pick up the spoon, aim it at the coffee pot, scoop up one level teaspoon of coffee and move it over the cup and empty the contents into the cup. Adding hot water is fraught with danger, as if I get the calculations wrong and miss the cup or tilt the kettle too vigorously, I will get burnt and may have to spend the day in the Accident and Emergency Department. Preparing to stir the drink, I need to calculate an appropriate force and velocity in order to avoid burning myself or spreading the drink over the floor. Now I just have to make my way back to my armchair!

Young children playing football together in the park need to constantly assess the speed and direction of incoming passes, whilst calculating the speed and direction of their own run, so as to arrange to be in the right place to receive the pass. Nobody without an undergraduate degree in mathematics could get these sums right, and they would need a pen and paper, as well as a calculator and the ball would be under a bus by the time that they had completed the calculation. Yet most children instinctively know the speed and direction of the run that they need to make in order to receive the ball.

Children are born weak and feeble, capable only of laying on their back and twitching uncontrollably. If placed next to a food source they will suckle and this has inevitable and uncontrolled consequences at either end of their young bodies.

By the time that they go to primary school five years later, they must be able to leave their parents behind, look after themselves, engage with staff and fellow students in meaningful discussion, comply with all reasonable directions and participate in drawing, colouring, writing or keyboarding as well as in elementary PE lessons.

By the time that they go to secondary school, 11 years after they were born, they are expected to participate in wide academic, cultural and PE programs. Today, it is not impossible for a few young children to even start becoming parents at this age, with all that this entails.

There has long been a debate as to whether this rapid development is a result of nature or nurture. Clearly, both have a fundamental role to play. While there is little that ordinary parents can do to improve on nature, there is a great deal that parents can do to nurture their children, from taking them to the swimming pool, to arranging violin lessons, to teaching them foreign languages, to feeding only a well-balanced diet and enforcing a sensible bedtime.

Over the last 100 years, parents, teachers and doctors have all come to recognize that some children's movement skills are not developing as well as they did in previous generations. A wide range of specialists have addressed this problem and each specialist has proposed a solution that is within their own subject area. Put simply, if you consult a physician then the solution to your problem is likely to involve taking medication; if you consult a surgeon then the solution is very likely to involve surgery; but medication and surgery should only be resorted to as the last resort, especially in children.

There is now a growing consensus among many specialists that what is required in order to improve the movement skills of young children is a program of strenuous exercise, such as was indulged in by previous generations, but which is now overlooked by parents worried by news of paedophiles or just too busy to find time to take their children to the local sports centre.

Research has proved that children who experience difficulty in controlling their movements are appreciably weaker than those who do not, and that when this strength deficiency has undergone remedial exercise the movement difficulties have been resolved in 72 per cent of cases.

This does not come as a surprise to scientists working in this area. Considerable research has been undertaken in recent years, which has shown that strength training has a positive effect on the symptoms of cerebral palsy, Down's syndrome, Parkinson's disease, muscular dystrophy, multiple sclerosis, motor neurone disease and many other similar conditions.

Talking about children doing strength training used to worry parents, but we are not talking here about children lifting big heavy metal weights above their heads. We are talking about getting your child to do as much as the most active child in his or her class, no more. As a result your child will not become a strongman or woman, but will become as strong as the most active child in his or her class.

However, whilst 72 per cent improvement is an excellent result, it is not the total solution and after the eight-week exercise program, a second eight-week program aimed at improving the child's movement planning (praxis) is undertaken.

When the children then follow the remedial exercise program with further work to assist their praxis (movement planning) the movement difficulties have been shown to have been resolved in 87 per cent of cases.

Lifetime motor development

Research has shown that human movement starts before we are born, early in pregnancy. As we saw in the introduction, there is anecdotal evidence from expectant mothers that those babies who experience movement difficulties in childhood may be identified by their lack of early movement in the womb, so movement difficulties may start very early in our development, but this requires further research for confirmation (Kirby and Drew 2003).

Movement changes throughout our lives. Our bodies increase in length, girth, weight, proportion, muscle tone and strength as we develop in our youth and similarly these factors diminish in our declining years (Dick 2003). Our environment constantly changes, with changes in temperature, precipitation and lighting all affecting our perception. The objects with which we have to deal change in size, shape and velocity, changing our perspective and judgement.

> Every day, you move. This doesn't happen in a vacuum, though. Every movement you make occurs within the environment that surrounds you. You also move for a purpose – the tasks you perform have specific requirements. The way

you move now has changed a great deal from your earliest movements, and will keep changing throughout your life. This is the essence of the study of motor development.

(Haywood and Getchell 2005, p.x)

The fundamental nature of these effects is brought home to us by old age or by injury, when an assumed skill, learned half a century earlier, becomes impossible as a result of infirmity or a head injury. A task as simple as walking can become a problem when the surface on which we are walking changes.

Our arms and legs move in different and distinct ways when we walk on a concrete sidewalk and when we walk on an icy sidewalk – or on a sandy beach. However, although the actual movements may differ, the motor skill we perform in each of these different situations is walking.

(Magill 2003, p.4)

This quotation highlights the complexity of human movement and the importance of the calculations being made in the brain in order to walk from one surface to another, to move from concrete to sandy beach. If you read a biomechanics book you will discover the high level of mathematics involved in making these calculations. By the age of five, most children in the UK have started playing sports games such as football, cricket, netball or rounders. In football the players are required to run, dribble, pass, tackle, shoot and head the ball and interact with 21 other players, a ball and a referee. In cricket one has to be able to bat, bowl and field. Bowling requires you to run up and 'throw' a ball 22 yards so that it lands in the same small area every time. To field requires you to be able to run and catch a ball before it lands or chase it and stop it before it goes over the boundary. To bat requires you to assess the speed, direction, spin and movement in the air of a small ball coming towards you at great speed and strike it with a cricket bat. The levels of skill required in netball and rounders are broadly the same as football and cricket. In five years the child has made substantial progress in his or her movement skills. It is at about this time, as the child reaches five years of age, that parents and teachers start to notice the differing movement skills of children. As they begin to leave the family where they have been playing with siblings older and younger than themselves who may well possess similar movement skills, they go to school where they are compared to the other children in the area. This is the age when the most children with movement difficulties are sent for specialist movement assessment.

Individual difference factors that can contribute to differences in people's movement are:

- abilities

- attitudes

- body type

- cultural background

- emotional makeup

- fitness level

- learning style

- maturational level

- motivational level

- previous social experiences

- prior movement experiences.

  (Reprinted, with permission, from Schmidt and Wrisberg 2008, p.163)

Human babies are born very small, very weak, out of proportion and unable to move in any controlled or planned manner. If they are to play organized games with their friends by the age of five they clearly need to grow taller, heavier and stronger and to learn a number of movement skills. If they want to continue to play games like football and cricket into secondary school they will have to maintain these skills at the same time as their bodies are changing in size, strength and proportion and as they are learning new, more advanced skills.

Landmarks of achievement in movement skills have been identified for babies and children until they reach the age of 12 years, which is about the average age at which they undergo puberty and reach young adulthood. The areas of achievement considered include:

- fine motor control

- gross motor control

- speech language skills

- cognitive/perceptual skills

- perceptual/social skills.

  (Kurtz 2008)

These landmarks are set out in full in Table 3.1. Tracking of a child's performance in movement skills against these landmarks permits an assessment of his or her movement skills.

We need to move in order to feed ourselves or to reproduce, to move away from predators or to find heat and cool, light and shade, friends and family and all those other things that we need or want. At birth we are small and unable to move in any way, even by rolling. We are totally dependent on our parents and require them to do everything for us. As soon as we are born we start to seek ways in which we can influence our environment. We learn that to cry brings an adult to attend to our needs. We learn that by gripping an adult's finger we can secure his or her complete attention. Movement starts to improve our situation.

Movement is a complex activity, requiring the coordination of physical and neural functions. From a purely physical aspect, it requires bones, lined with cartilage to reduce friction whilst moving, held together with ligaments, moved by muscles attached to the bones by tendons. Lack of muscle tone and weakness, particularly in the muscles of the hands and wrists has been shown to be a symptom of dyspraxia, as we have seen (Oliveira *et al.* 2006). No literature has been found that proposes or investigates any physical difficulties other than muscular strength, which may cause movement difficulties, in children and the possibilities are not pursued here. The neural functions which control movement are complex. According to Macintyre moving well involves:

- controlling the body as it moves

- coordinating different body parts so that movement is smooth

- gauging the correct amount of strength and speed

- understanding directionality

- being able to manipulate objects

- appreciating the rhythm of movements to aid repetition

- making safety decisions about when to move and where to move, and

- being able to stay still!

(Macintyre 2002, p.2)

Summary

The perfect child has yet to be born. We each have defects and weaknesses that can be improved by exercise, training and experience of life. Good parents guide their child's development by arranging a healthy lifestyle and challenging developmental activities.

Physical development includes a range of activities ranging from endurance exercise that develops the heart and lungs to some form of gentle strength training. The success or failure of this work can be seen by comparing your child with their peers.

A lack of strength training will not only prevent your child from becoming a weightlifter, but will make any involvement in sport difficult. In the worst cases it may result in movement difficulties that cause them to go around home and school knocking over the furniture and result in relationship problems with their peers.

Chapter 5

Why the Program Works

What doesn't kill you makes you stronger.

(Paraphrased by Nietzsche 1888)

Introduction

In previous chapters it has been shown that in the last century children have participated in less exercise and that their fitness and movement skills have deteriorated as a result.

Modern exercise programs

Patterns of physical activity in young children have also changed fundamentally in the last century (Washington *et al.* 2001). Self-determined and self-regulated free play (Schraw, Crippen and Hartley 2006) has almost completely disappeared due to a range of social, cultural and lifestyle changes that have taken place during this period. Only a belief, largely unsupported by scientific evidence, that the health and fitness of our young people will be affected by a lack of exercise (Rowland 2007) and the need for healthy recruits to the armed forces, has stemmed the decline. Parents, keen to ensure the health and fitness of their children, are arranging for them to participate in competitive sports (Washington *et al.* 2001) such as football, rugby, basketball and martial arts, where they will be protected, encouraged and coached by trained and approved professional staff. Simultaneously, as we have seen, the levels of fitness and the quality of the movement skills of our young people have troubled commentators (Baden-Powell 1908; *British Medical Journal* 1962; Nordau 1892).

It is widely recognized that free play by children allows for the development of motor skills (Piaget 1962 in Rowland 2007; Washington *et al.* 2001). Children need to learn a range of key movement skills in their early years, including throwing, catching, kicking and hitting a ball. These skills need to be learned at definite stages of each child's development and do not develop sooner simply as a result of introducing them to children at an earlier age (Branta *et al.* 1984 in Washington *et al.* 2001). They have traditionally been learned whilst participating in free play with the lessons reinforced during school PE classes. Unfortunately, the reduction in time spent on free play has coincided with school PE programs diminishing in duration and content (Washington *et al.* 2001) and as no competitive sport includes all of these skills, the skills are deteriorating. It is also necessary to consider the motivational factors acting on the children in play.

The informal nature of free play arouses many of the positive factors of variety, freedom and fun and permits a focus on success without the need to acknowledge failure. The more formal competitive sports must include a certain amount of regimentation and competition that can lead to acknowledgement of failure and embarrassment and, with poor coaching, can lead to boredom and injury.

There are few similarities between free play and competitive sport. Children can engage in free play at any time including that time before their parents get up and when they are at work. Historically, children went out after breakfast and were told to return for their evening meal. In order to participate in organized, competitive sport, facilities have to be hired and professional coaches paid, so sessions are likely to be limited to just one or two hours. In free play children keep going until their exhaustion overtakes their enthusiasm, whilst in competitive sport professional coaches encourage and even enforce regular breaks. Free play involves a wide variety of activities partly due to its duration and anecdotal evidence suggests that it often included wrestling, lifting, throwing and climbing. These are not popular competitive sports, and participation in them is likely to have diminished and if this is the case then the strength of the children is likely to diminish also.

Replacing free play with competitive sport is likely to introduce a number of other changes relating to the nature of the particular sport selected. The *frequency* of each session is likely to be restricted if adult coaches have to be paid at an hourly rate. The *intensity* of each session is likely to be restricted by cautious adult coaches. The *time* that each session is likely to last is likely to be restricted if adult coaches have to be paid at an hourly rate. The *type* of training is likely to be decided by the parents who arrange for the child to attend or by the adult coach supervising the session in the case of general sessions. Frequency, intensity, time and type combine to form the FITT principle used to assess the effectiveness of fitness training (Walker 2004).

Fitness in young people
The result of this caution is the reduction in the fitness levels of our children that is the focus of a great deal of government attention.

The government response was to set a minimum of two hours' participation in high-quality PE for all children in 2002, and to announce in 2007 an additional £100m campaign to give every child the opportunity to participate in five hours of sport every week, but time for PE and sport is only a small part of the solution.

Children today are overweight, lacking in strength and endurance and do not possess the movement skills of their ancestors. Their life expectancy, quality of life, health, education and fitness are all doomed to suffer as a result. It is a frightening prospect and one that is currently prompting a great deal of government action and investment, mainly focused on increasing children's level of activity.

The solution

In comparison with PE lessons, children sent out to play unsupervised are naturally competitive and derive great pleasure from competing against their peers in any game or activity.

The solution is to combine the features of PE with the principles of unsupervised play, to produce what will be referred to here as 'feral play'. It is supervised with a light hand, involves all the principles of competition that motivate children, is great fun and improves strength and endurance explosively. Involving vigorous exercise as it does, it may even improve body composition and movement skills.

When these rules were applied by a sports coach during recent research they clearly excited the class teachers with the opportunities to help the children make real progress with their fitness and skills, but they also caused them a degree of professional embarrassment (senior managers in schools demand strict discipline and silence and it is now recognized that this severely inhibits children so as to restrict their performance and improvement in sport and PE) and it was eventually agreed that the classes would be run by the sports coach with the assistance of the class learning support assistant. However, many members of staff, several of them specialist PE staff, observed that the children looked forward to the lessons, exerted themselves strenuously during the lessons and upon their return to class told stories of their experiences in the classes. Many of the children asked when the classes would re-start. During informal conversations, members of staff have reported that the children's behaviour showed a marked improvement following these classes, once they had settled down after the excitement of the class. At least one of the schools which participated in the research has changed its policy in relation to the reporting for accidents, as a result of staff experience during the research.

In order to formalize the definition of 'feral play' and to encourage teachers and sports leaders at schools to experiment with it, the following guidelines have been produced.

Feral play

Feral play refers to the way that children used to amuse themselves in decades gone by. It relates to the uncontrolled, unrestrained way in which children used to play when let out of the house to meet up with friends and only return in time for their evening meal.

Feral play is physical, competitive activity. No breaks are taken for refreshment, drinks, toilet or even injury. It requires, and develops great strength, endurance, fitness, coordination, movement skills and self-confidence.

In its natural form, feral play does not involve adults, but the involvement of adults does not, in itself, prevent feral play from taking place, provided that the adult involvement does not become authoritarian, intrusive or break any of the other rules.

1. Supervised feral play should be limited to 30-minute sessions and start with a drink and use of the toilet, so that later requests for breaks may be safely declined.

2. The usual safety requirement for the environment, the equipment and the athletes (injury and dress) to be checked can be observed before the children arrive.

3. Simple safety rules, such as 'no go areas', are rigidly enforced. This may involve gymnasium equipment, etc. These should be kept to a minimum and may develop over time. Breach requires a short exclusion, maybe two minutes.

4. Any violence, physical confrontation, breach of the rules or cheating requires a warning before a short exclusion, maybe two minutes, if repeated.

5. The adult should imitate a rugby union referee as closely as possible, by constantly giving out instructions and naming offenders and giving personal instructions in order to gain compliance.

6. All unnecessary limits and restraints are avoided.

7. All injuries are ignored for one minute. Without attention most children will be keen to resume the activity. A little blood or a bruise or a sting will be forgotten in the heat of the moment.

8. All activities are based on competition and competition is encouraged as a positive activity.

9. The adult must be enthusiastic, relaxed and possess a long and varied list of challenging activities.

10. All sessions must end with a drink and use of the toilet, as no breaks will have been permitted during the session.

Progressive resistance training

The value of progressive resistance training in developing a healthy body has long been recognized by young men all over the world. According to Greek mythology, Milo of Croton (a wrestler from the sixth century BC) trained by lifting and carrying a newborn calf on his back every day. After two years the calf had become a cow and Milo had become a weightlifter (Pomeroy *et al.* 2009). Irrespective of the veracity of the story, it vividly sets out the principles and value of progressive resistance training. Soon a number of scientists became interested in the subject of strength training. Hippocrates (460–370 BC), the father of modern medicine, recommended it to his patients (Pomeroy *et al.* 2009). Another Greek, Galen of Pergamum (AD 129–199), who was given the position of personal physician to several emperors and whose theories dominated and influenced Western medical science for well over a millennium, recommended strength training exercises using an early form of dumbbell called halteres (Pomeroy *et al.* 2009).

The application of the principles of progressive resistance training in strength training programs has continued to increase through the ages. In 1955, Oscar State and Geoff Dyson published a book entitled *Weight Training for Athletics* (State 1955). It introduced the concept of weight training to the wide variety of running, jumping and throwing events in athletics in order to improve performance. This book started an expansion in strength training in sport that culminated in 1988 in the East German Olympic Committee announcing a policy that required athletes from every Olympic sport except sailing to undertake a program of progressive resistance training. In 1996 the United States Olympic Committee published a similar policy.

Traditionally, the lifting of heavy weights has had a reputation for being dangerous and unhealthy (Department of Education and Science 1980; Rugby Football Union 1990). Weights are excellent tools for promoting substantial physiological changes to the human body such as improved strength and increased muscle bulk, but accidents can occur when weights are not secured to bars and when weights are used without spotters. However, whilst the lifting of heavy weights clearly creates the potential for serious accidents to occur, records show that relatively few accidents actually occur and that relatively few people are injured in weights rooms so that weightlifting is one of the safest sports (Hamill 1994; Zatsiorsky and Kraemer 2006). Weights rooms are like physiotherapy departments in that they contain much of the same equipment: bars, discs, collars, dumbbells, multigyms and medicine balls. The recognition of the potential risks and the enforcement of strict discipline in both the physiotherapy department and the weights room, ranging from dress codes to rules governing personal behaviour and the use of the equipment, have eliminated the risks.

Historically the use of weights by women and young men has provoked considerable debate. It has been said that women will grow bigger and more muscled and that young men will injure their epiphyseal plates and stunt their growth (Zatsiorsky and Kraemer 2006) and lose flexibility and become musclebound (Stratton et al. 2004). There is now an almost universal acceptance amongst sports scientists and medical staff that resistance training is safe for all ages and both genders and that all the identified risks from lifting weights can be resolved by high quality professional coaching. A number of high profile, respected bodies have published policy statements on resistance training for young people which confirm these views (Behm et al. 2008; Faigenbaum et al. 1996; Stratton et al. 2004). Several of the leading authors on strength training have now published books promoting the subject (Faigenbaum and Westcott 2000;

Kraemer and Fleck 1993). It is interesting to note that the person voted the best weightlifter of the twentieth century and the first person to clean and jerk three times his bodyweight was a 16-year-old boy. Naim Suleymanov won Olympic Gold Medals in 1988, 1992 and 1996, when he was refereed by the author of this book.

The science of strength training

The scientific principles upon which strength training is founded are simple and basic but for completeness and in recognition that not all readers will have a sports science background they are set out below:

- strength

- endurance

- fitness

- speed

- flexibility

- body composition.

The components are very closely related and this relationship is illustrated in Figure 5.1:

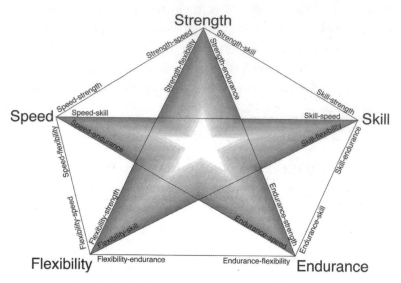

Figure 5.1: The relationship between the components of fitness
(Stone, Stone and Sands 2007, p.4)

The Principles of Training (the principles on which all sports training must be based if progress is to be made) state that in order to improve fitness, all training must be:

- progressive

- overload

- varied

- planned

- specific

- reversible.

All strength training programs must follow these principles in order to increase strength in any person.

Chapter 6

Exercises and Session Plans for Strength and Fitness

The sessions that we are proposing are designed to improve fitness and strength in the same way that children would improve their fitness and strength if left to play unsupervised with their friends.

'Fitness' is the ability to recover after a training load. It is important because it helps to develop the heart and lungs.

'Strength' is the ability to lift heavy objects or to overcome a resistance.

These sessions are not designed to build great strength, but rather to eliminate exceptional weakness and ensure that children with dyspraxia are no weaker than their average classmates. Research has shown that children with dyspraxia are weaker than their peers (Raynor 1989; Raynor 2001). This weakness has been shown to be due in part to the fact that children with dyspraxia do not have the same ability as their peers to activate their muscles efficiently and because sometimes they coactivate, which means that they activate the muscles in pairs, so that they activate the muscles that straighten the leg at the same time as activating the muscles that bend the leg, so that these muscles cancel each other out (Platt 2010).

The program has been designed to require minimal equipment and minimal supervision. A gym floor with a gymnasium bench or a flat field with a tree log is all that is required. A parent, teacher or sports coach, with no qualifications can supervise any session.

Equipment

These sessions have been designed so that almost no equipment is necessary to run them. A piece of flat, level ground approximately 20 metres (66 feet) long is ideal. Take off your jumpers to mark the strip that you are going to use. This marks your territory and means carrying less equipment. The only other equipment that is needed is a bench or log about 25 cm (10 inches) high and stable, that can be used to jump on and off. If you cannot find something suitable take your time as the first few sessions can be an easy introduction whilst you find the bench or log. A tennis and/or squash ball is useful if you have one as this will help to improve the child's grip.

If the weather permits it is always nicer to exercise outside, where there is fresh air and a chance to commune with nature, although the presence of large, aggressive dogs and too many observers should be avoided, particularly at the start.

Clothing

Remember that children with dyspraxia are reluctant to take part in physical activity and it may be better, at least when starting the program, not to make a big deal out of getting changed into a fancy tracksuit and trainers. It may be better to keep to some old clothes that permit free movement and that you will not be worried to see get dirty or even torn. If these clothes are put on a couple of hours before the planned session it makes less of a deal of going training and children can go as they are and therefore be more relaxed about the session.

Shoes

Suitable footwear is more important than clothing, but nowadays most children consider trainers to be fashion accessories rather than sports equipment. Firm support and good grip are essential for running, jumping and hopping, which all put the foot under a little pressure. Again these can be put on a couple of hours before the session, so that going training is no big deal.

Changing

As the children become more used to participating in these sessions then it may be easier to get changed at the venue. Make sure that the children always have a good drink of water and always use the toilet. Remember that children with dyspraxia do not like taking part in physical activity and that they know that repeated requests to use the toilet or to get a drink will break up the session. As the session is only half an hour, there should be absolutely no toilet or drinks breaks. No healthy child needs to drink more than once in half an hour and they will drink at the start and at the finish of the session. Similarly, no healthy child needs to use the toilet more than once in half an hour and they will be encouraged to use the toilet at the start and finish of the session.

Gently encourage your child to ignore an injury that you did not see happen and for which you can see no consequences. Children enjoy the attention that they receive from you if they report an injury, however minor. Children have low pain thresholds and if something really hurts no amount of gentle encouragement will compel them to continue. You must then make a point of seeking them out 60 seconds later to ask how the injury feels. By this time most children will have forgotten the injury and be happy to continue. If they are not, treat the injury.

Supervision

Remember that you are responsible for all aspects of your child's safety. You should check the area that you propose to use for any broken glass, thorns or nettles, and so forth. Check any equipment that you propose to use during the session. Check your child for injuries and illnesses and that they are wearing suitable clothing and footwear. Make sure that you have a basic first aid kit for any little cuts, bruises or stings. Take a suitable sunscreen along if working outside.

The exercises
Running
This is a simple activity, familiar to all children. There is no need to focus on the technique unless you feel that there is a serious problem with it.

Figure 6.1: Running

Hopping
Another simple activity, familiar to all children. This adds variety to the session and keeps the children thinking as well as exercising. Hop right foot up the track and hop left foot back down the track.

Figure 6.2: Hopping

Jumping

Put two feet together and jump along the track. Some children find it a little difficult to keep their feet together whilst jumping to start with, but they all pick it up very quickly if given time. Vary this exercise by making each jump as long as you can or by touching the ground with both hands between jumps. These variations make the child work their legs a little harder.

Figure 6.3: Jumping

Figure 6.4: Jumping and touching the floor

Bench stepping

Stand on top of the bench. Jump down onto the ground, with one foot either side of the bench. Jump up onto the bench again. Repeat this 20 times.

Stand on top of the bench.	Jump down onto the ground, with one foot either side of the bench.	Jump up onto the bench again.

Figure 6.5: Bench stepping

Bench jumping

Repeat this exercise ten times at a good pace.

Stand on top of the bench.	Jump down onto the ground, with one foot either side of the bench.	Sit down on the bench.

Figure 6.6: Bench jumping

Crush the ball

Repeat this exercise ten times.

Pass the ball to the other hand and crush it as tight as you can ten times.

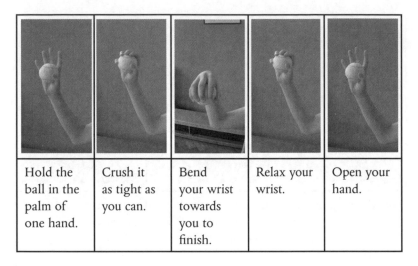

Hold the ball in the palm of one hand.	Crush it as tight as you can.	Bend your wrist towards you to finish.	Relax your wrist.	Open your hand.

Figure 6.7: Crush the ball

Children with dyspraxia have been found to have weak fingers, hands and wrists that may result in them experiencing difficulties in fine motor skills such as writing and drawing.

The Strength and Fitness Program
Week 1

1. Run up, walk back × 6.

2. Right foot hopping, walk back × 2 (for all, even those who are left-footed!).

3. Left foot hopping, walk back × 2.

4. Two-footed bunny hopping, walk back × 2.

The program starts with a session of races. Set up a track approximately 35 metres long. Encourage a competitive atmosphere in order to increase the intensity of the exercise. Keep to left and right foot irrespective of whether the child is right-handed or left-handed.

Week 2

1. Run up, walk back × 6.

2. Right foot hopping, walk back × 6.

3. Left foot hopping, walk back × 6.

4. Two-footed bunny hopping, walk back × 6.

The volume is increasing. This is not to reflect any improvement in the children's fitness, but just to familiarize them with doing more work. Increase the pace of the session.

Week 3

1. Run up, run back × 6.

2. One more race for winners of all the heats.

3. Right foot hopping, run back × 6.

4. Left foot hopping, run back × 6.

5. Two-footed bunny hopping (this time touch the ground between hops), run back × 6.

6. Bench jumping (Stage 1) × 10 × 2.

Adding a championship race at (2) increases the intensity of the session. Touching the ground between hops makes the child go into a deep knee bend and dramatically increase the intensity of the exercise.

Week 4

1. Run up, run back × 6.

2. One more race for winners of all the heats.

3. Relay race with class divided into two teams × 2.

4. Right foot hopping, run back × 6.

5. Left foot hopping, run back × 6.

6. Two-footed bunny hopping (this time touch the ground between hops), run back × 6.

7. Bench jumping (stage 1) × 10 × 6.

Adding the relay adds a little volume to the program, but considerably increases the intensity and the children get *really* motivated.

Week 5

1. Run up, run back × 6.

2. One more race for winners of all the heats.

3. Relay race with class divided into two teams × 2.

4. Right foot hopping, run back × 6.

5. Left foot hopping, run back × 6.

6. Two-footed bunny hopping (this time touch the ground between hops), run back × 6.

7. Bench jumping (stage 1) × 10 × 6.

8. Bench jumping (stage 2) × 10 × 2.

Week 6

1. Run up, run back × 6.

2. One more race for winners of all the heats.

3. Relay race with class divided into two teams × 2.

4. Right foot hopping, run back × 6.

5. Left foot hopping, run back × 6.

6. Two footed bunny hopping (this time touch the ground between hops), run back × 6.

7. Bench jumping (stage 2) × 10 × 6.

Now the real work starts with the stage 2 bench jumping!

Week 7

1. Run up, run back × 6.

2. One more race for winners of all the heats.

3. Relay race with class divided into two teams × 2.

4. Right foot hopping, run back × 6.

5. Left foot hopping, run back × 6.

6. Two-footed bunny hopping (this time touch the ground between hops), run back × 6.

7. Bench jumping (stage 2) × 10 × 9.

The work increases!

Week 8

1. Run up, run back × 6.

2. One more race for winners of all the heats.

3. Relay race with class divided into two teams × 2.

4. Right foot hopping, run back × 6.

5. Left foot hopping, run back × 6.

6. Two-footed bunny hopping (this time touch the ground between hops), run back × 6.

7. Bench jumping (stage 2) × 10 × 12.

We finish the hard work with a lot of bench jumping.

How often?

During their summer holidays, primary school children will play all day every day, if allowed to. I would recommend that they be allowed to participate in this program six days a week. This will allow them one day each week in order to recover from their exertions. By the time the children move to secondary school they can no longer manage to exercise six days and three or four days would be more appropriate.

How long?

Each session should last 30 minutes from the time that they start exercising until the time that they finish. As far as possible, there should be no breaks and no distractions during this time. Toilet breaks and drink breaks occur before and after the session and no healthy child needs to go for either more than every 30 minutes.

How intense is the session?

Primary school children can run continuously for well over an hour, so 30 minutes should be no problem for them. Let them go at their own pace, with sensible encouragement from you. Be careful not to drive them harder than they want to go. When you get a chance, go to a local park and watch children in self-directed play without parental intervention. The children work ten times harder than their PE teachers ask them to at school.

Recovery

After exercise, an athlete needs to complete three stages of recovery. The first is to re-hydrate, which is best achieved by taking sips of cool water from a bottle. Be careful not to drink too much too quickly or to drink ice cold water if you are warm after exercise. The second stage is to re-energize and this is best achieved with a piece of fruit or a handful of dried fruit. The third stage of recovery is to clear the lactic acid, which is the waste product from burning up all the energy during exercise. This is best done with a long warm shower, followed by a brisk rub down with a nice, rough towel.

Summary

A simple exercise program has been set down and explained that will bring the weaker child back to the level of strength of his or her peers. This should improve the efficiency of children's muscles so that they improve their movement skills to the level of the other children in their class.

Being a strengthening program, it is of short duration, but dynamic and vigorous.

Chapter 7

Exercises and Session Plans for Movement Planning

The following exercises have been designed to encourage children to practise their skills in planning movements, without any pressure or stress and with almost no consequences. The exercises are best done under the personal supervision of an adult in small groups, although they can be done on a one-to-one basis.

The exercises may be undertaken in the open, in a garden, park or field and there is little or no equipment required or planning necessary to make it happen. The adult needs to have a positive attitude and to support the child in every way. Every success needs to be recognized and strongly praised. Every failure needs to be brushed over.

Many of the exercises require the adult to set them at an appropriate level to the child's present level of skill so that they are a challenge, but so that the child is almost inevitably successful in every attempt. Only if this balance is correctly set will the children enjoy themselves enough to keep coming back and make the progress that they need to make in order to live a happy and successful life.

Movement Planning (Praxis) Training
Week 1

1. Bounding down the road × 12.

2. Throwing a ball against an uneven wall and catching it in both hands × 12.

These sessions are calm and controlled. They are about the children getting an opportunity to learn new skills and practice them. In order to achieve the results that they need, the children must not feel tired or stressed.

In the bounding session the adult spontaneously calls out 'hop right leg', 'hop left leg', 'step', 'bunny hop', etc. randomly, giving the children time to complete the movement and review it. The adult then gives positive feedback on each child's achievements.

Any child can throw a ball against a wall, but the throw needs to be controlled if the child is to have any chance of catching it using only his or her two hands, rather than trapping it between chest and arms. The uneven wall means that the ball bounces unevenly and this restricts the time that the child receives to respond to it.

Week 2

1. Bounding session × 12.

2. Throwing a ball against an uneven wall and catching it in both hands × 12.

The same session this week, but trying to make each task just a little more difficult, whilst still easily achievable. It is not our aim to humiliate the child or undermine self-confidence.

Week 3

1. Put down 'islands' that the child can step on when crossing the 'river'.

2. Use a tennis racquet to hit a ball thrown by a child.

Colour sheets of newspaper about twice the size of the child's foot so that these become 'islands' that the child aims to step on as they cross a 'river'. The sheets can be reduced in size and moved around in order to vary the difficulty of the task. The children need to work in order to succeed every time.

A tennis racquet has a large head and most children are familiar with them, so this is quite a simple task.

Week 4

1. Put down 'islands' that the child can step on when crossing the 'river'.

2. Use a tennis racquet to hit a ball thrown by a child.

The same session this week, but trying to make each task just a little more difficult, whilst still easily achievable. It is not our aim to humiliate the child or undermine self-confidence.

Week 5

1. Running over six hurdles × 12.

2. Use a baseball bat to hit a ball thrown by a child.

It is possible to buy small hurdles, about 6 inches/15 cm high, which fall over if you hit them, or you can use small cardboard boxes that crumple if you step on them. Place the hurdles at unusual and irregular distances apart so that the child has to think carefully about their foot placements.

Few children are familiar with a rounders or baseball bat and it has a much smaller head, which makes the task considerably tougher.

Week 6

1. Running over six hurdles × 12.

2. Use a baseball bat to hit a ball thrown by an adult.

As the children improve, bring the hurdles very close together, or make them further apart.

Adults can throw the ball with a little swing or spin, to make the task a little more difficult.

Week 7

1. Run down the road (but you cannot take a step until you touch your foot with the opposite hand).

2. Juggling down the road. Hold a tennis ball in each hand. Step with one foot and throw and catch the ball in the same hand and repeat.

The children are now going to cross their midline and use right foot and left leg and vice versa. Allow the child to walk as slowly as they need to when starting this task and then encourage them to speed up a little as they improve.

Juggling down the road, the child holds a ball in each hand and takes a step. He or she then stops and throws the ball in the same hand as the foot just 6 inches/15 cm into the air and catches it in the same hand. Then take a step with the other hand and stop and throw that ball into that hand and so on.

Week 8

1. Run down the road (but you cannot take a step until you touch your foot with the hand on the same side).

2. Juggling down the road. Hold a tennis ball in each hand. Step with one foot and throw and catch the ball in the hand on the same side and repeat.

This is the final, ultimate week and the tasks are very complex. Touching the foot with the hand on the same side does not cross the midline, so it would appear simpler than the alternative, but it does mean that the same leg and arm are moving, which undermines the child's balance.

Allow the children to move as slowly as they want to whilst they start to understand the task and its challenges. They can speed up later as their skills improve.

Summary
The two stages of the program have now resolved almost all of the symptoms of dyspraxia. The first stage of the program was the strength training program that eliminated the muscular

weakness that symptomizes dyspraxia and the second stage of the program was the praxis training that made up for the lack of skills as a result of the lack of sports practice.

Chapter 8

What You Can Do to Support a Child During the Sessions

Safety

Young children have a tremendous capacity to perform strenuous exercise for long periods. They do not have, however, the mental strength to continue beyond what they can safely do and they are, therefore, unable to hurt themselves by training too hard. There are just two threats to children when exercising. The first of these is allowing children to exercise outside in the sun, when they may quickly suffer from sunstroke and therefore need to cover themselves with clothing or sun lotion. The second risk is from a failure to drink sufficient quantities of water, as children have no ability to judge their own hydration or their own need to take fluids.

Children are, however, perfectly capable of avoiding strenuous exercise. They will frequently leave the changing room for the gym and immediately seek permission to return to the changing room in order to use the toilet or have a drink. By supervising the children whilst they are changing, it is possible to ensure that every child takes a drink and uses the toilet before leaving, so removing the need for them to return during the class.

Children will also report fictional injuries so that they can enjoy some one-to-one time with a teacher or other adult. As a rule, such requests should be refused unless the incident which caused the injury was witnessed or there is a flow of blood. The child should then be asked about the injury 60 seconds later, when they will frequently have forgotten it.

This book is about helping children to overcome a difficulty that they are experiencing. Parents and teachers are essential to achieving the goals of the session but they should try to play down their involvement as much as possible.

The primary purpose of the parent or guardian is to protect the children. A session in which you bring back the same number of children that you take, and avoid a stop off at the local hospital even if the children don't get to exercise, is a better one than the session where the children achieve all their exercise goals but just one child gets injured or lost.

Avoid becoming involved in the details of the session and keep focused on the overall strategic picture of what is going on. The success of the session does not depend on you setting out the cones as there are children around who would be flattered to be asked to help you to set them out. Stand in the middle of the park and direct operations and make sure that the cones are put where you need them to be.

From your position in the middle of the park you can see all the children and you can see any that are drifting away from you as well as anybody who is approaching the group. Keep counting the children every couple of minutes. It is very easy to keep a watchful eye over a group of children and to take pleasure in how well everything is going and then realize that you haven't seen little Johnny for half an hour.

You will only have control of what is happening if everybody can hear you. There is a modern view that volume is not important in coaching sport, but the children cannot do what you want them to do if they don't know what you want them to do. If you don't want to shout, then take a whistle.

There will need to be enough adults for the number of children that you are taking. Whilst one adult can control 30 children in a classroom, the number is far less without those walls to restrain the children. Remember that children cannot simply be allowed to go off on their own to the toilet or to get a drink, so there will need to be adults available to supervise these activities.

Remember that the law requires checks to be made on adults working with children to ensure their suitability to do so.

Be aware of any adults that get close to the group and act to prevent them getting too close or too involved with your children.

The 'trick' is to anticipate any problems as early as possible and to act promptly to remove any risks or threats. The longer you fail to act, then the worse the situation is likely to get. You don't usually have to take dramatic action, but don't ignore situations.

Your venue

Visit your venue and have a look around before you arrange to take half the children in the neighbourhood down there. Perhaps, take your own children with you. Let them run around. If they find the potholes and the dog poo this time it will save a lot of problems next time.

Take a piece of paper and a pencil with you. Draw a map of the site and illustrate the local toilets, the coffee shop and such places. Mark the car park and how far it is to walk to the spot that you have chosen. The map doesn't have to be a work of art as long as you can read it and understand it.

Mark a point where parents or ambulances can meet you in case of emergency. Practise explaining to an emergency operator where you want the ambulance sent because next time a child might be bleeding when you have to do this. A useful tip is to select a rendezvous point which is close at hand and easily found by the ambulance crew who may not know the area. Remember that most fields don't have street names and numbers, and asking the ambulance crew to find the third oak tree on the left may leave you waiting a long time for them to find you.

Equipment

As any parent will tell you, even the simplest activity session requires you to take a considerable amount of equipment.

It is difficult to justify not taking a first aid kit with you when you are taking other people's children to play in a park. A few plasters and a couple of dressings are better than nothing. A qualified first aider is ideal, but confidence in your ability to deal with simple cuts and bruises is essential.

A mobile telephone allows you to call for help if things go wrong and you need the police to chase off troublesome youth or the ambulance service to take a child who fell onto broken glass to hospital. Check that the telephone works where you are going. You will need signal, battery strength and credit for it to work. Sometimes a mobile telephone will work on one side of a football pitch, but not on the other side, and it is not good policy to wait until you need to use it to find out where it works. Do not allow yourself to become distracted by answering calls yourself, however important they may seem at the time. Your task now is looking after the children.

A list of the names of the children and the contact numbers of their parents or guardians allows you to summon adults to take troublesome children home or to inform the relatives of injured children. The more numbers that you have the better and the more up to date they are the better. You will never realize the value of this list until something goes wrong!

Although some parents may be reluctant to supply you with a medical history of their child for the first session, if you are taking the same children regularly then you may like to find out any who have conditions that could cause you problems, such as diabetes, epilepsy and asthma. As long as you are aware of the children with these conditions, then you can familiarize yourself with the treatment and what the parent wants you to do should the child need help. (Johnny has a little blue inhaler in his pocket and two puffs are usually enough; a carbonated drink usually puts him right, etc.)

As previously stated, nobody can follow your instructions if they can't hear them. If you cannot shout loud enough or don't like to do so, then you will need a whistle and everybody will need to know what you want them to do when you blow it. For example, 'The simplest system is for everybody to stop and look at me when I blow the whistle and I will give you a hand signal of what I want you to do. Alternatively, one blow means stop, two blows mean…'

Plastic cones allow you to mark out the area that you are using for the session. Nobody leaves this area without your permission. Remember as the person in charge you must be able to say where every child is at every minute. Cones can be almost as valuable as the walls in a classroom if properly used.

You will need to take food and drink along to the session. A bottle of fresh water is required for very hot days and is useful for washing lumps of mud out of cuts. Keep a non-return valve on the top of the bottle if possible. You may well find that one or two of the children are diabetic and may need calories urgently if exercising. This is not a problem as long as you can give them something. Cans of carbonated drinks are ideal for this purpose. You can open them, tip some away and then shake the contents to dispose of the gas and then you are left with a very sugary drink that is ideal for diabetics. Sugar lumps, dextrose tablets or candy bars are also useful. Chocolate is good but can get very messy on sunny or warm days.

Remain calm

This chapter has set out a number of steps that need to be taken in order to avoid problems that may occur and to deal with any that do occur. You should not allow this to intimidate you or deter you from the plans that you have set down. These are simple precautions to avoid things that can go wrong and most can be achieved in a few minutes. Hopefully, you will organize these sessions for years and never have any problems, but it would be stupid not to prepare for the worst.

On the day

Develop a positive mental attitude: this is going to be fun! Fun for my child. Fun for the other children. Fun for me.

Try to be available well before the session is due to start, so that you are relaxed and not rushing. Have everything ready so that nothing can go wrong. Read through your checklist one more time.

Checklist

- Check the times that the park is open.

- Check the times that you and your child are available.

- Give eight hours' notice of the session to your child so that he or she can prepare him- or herself.

- Ensure that your child is suitably dressed for the session well before it is time to go, so that the session is no big deal.

- Make sure that your child has suitable trainers or footwear on well before it is time to go.

- Ensure that you have a piece of fruit or a handful of dried fruit and a bottle of water for your child when he or she finishes training.

- Make sure that you have a session plan for the session. If you keep a book in the car with a record of previous sessions then a brief note can be made after the sessions and minor adjustments made for next time.

- Take a change of clothing in case of rain.

- Have fun and get home as soon as possible.

- Remember that you are here because your child experiences difficulties in doing this.

- Do not expect world records. Acknowledge every achievement. Praise him or her frequently.

It is about taking your children down to the park to play. The task should be fun for both parent and child; a chance for some one-to-one time.

If you have other children, then arrange the sessions to take place when somebody else can look after them. You are there to focus on the child with dyspraxia and to help him or her overcome his or her problem. No good at all will come from trying to take two or three children to the park at the same time. You cannot focus on two or three children at the same time and the sessions will have no value.

If either of you feel that this is a burden then the sessions will soon stop. Neither of you will want to spend time under pressure and under stress. Make the sessions short, sharp and fun. Don't let it drag out into an hour or two by adding games of football and so on. Arrange other trips to the park for that. Let this session be fast, enjoyable and then go home.

Do not worry about trying to become a sports coach in order to help your child to perform better. It is not necessary.

You should start to notice an improvement in your child's movement skills by the end of the sixth week and the best improvements will then come over the next six weeks.

The principles that govern the session are the principles of good parenting.

For those parents who are new to coaching sport, it may be useful to consider what we are trying to achieve, what the children may expect and work out a philosophy for our work and for this reason the Bill of Rights and key points are included.

Bill Of Rights for Young Athletes

- Right to participate in sports

- Right to participate at a level commensurate with each child's maturity and ability

- Right to have qualified adult leadership

- Right to play as a child and not as an adult

- Right of children to share in the leadership and decision-making of their sport participation

- Right to participate in safe and healthy environments

- Right to proper preparation for participation in sports

- Right to an equal opportunity to strive for success

- Right to be treated with dignity

- Right to have fun in sports.

(Reprinted, with permission, from Martens, R., Christina, R.W., Harvey, J.S., and Sharkey, B.J. 1981, Coaching Young Athletes Champaign, IL: Human Kinetics, p.7)

Key points to remember

- Athletes are motivated to play sports to fulfill their need for fun and to feel worthy.

- People have a need for an optimal amount of arousal.

- When optimally aroused, the 'flow experience' is more likely to occur.

- You can help athletes experience optimal arousal and thus flow by fitting the difficulty of the skill to the ability of the athlete, keeping practices varied and all players active, and avoiding continually instructing and evaluating your athletes.

- Sports are potentially threatening to young athletes because they equate their achievement with their self-worth.

- Success-oriented athletes see winning as a consequence of their ability, blaming failure on insufficient effort.

- Failure-oriented athletes attribute losing to a lack of ability and infrequent wins to luck, thus blaming themselves for losing and yet not taking credit for winning.

- Failure-oriented athletes attempt to protect their self-worth by putting forth only token effort so others will not discover their feared lack of ability. Coaches often mistake this lack of effort as a lack of motivation, but in actuality, failure-oriented athletes are highly motivated to avoid the threat to their self-worth.

- Coaches develop expectancies of athletes which, when conveyed, may become self-fulfilling prophesies.

- Failure-oriented athletes are most vulnerable to coaches' negative expectancies.

- Athletes learn to fear failure because:

  a.   the mistakes and errors that are a natural part of the learning process are misinterpreted as failures;

  b.   competitive pressures result in youngsters setting unrealistically high goals which assure failure;

  c.   athletes begin playing for extrinsic rewards rather than to attain personal goals.

- The most important thing you can do to enhance your athletes' motivation is to teach them that success means achieving their personal performance goals rather than the performance goals of others.

- You can play a vital role in helping athletes to set realistic goals. Realistic goals are those that motivate athletes to achieve their finest but to recognize their limitations as well.

- Athletes perform best when they are optimally aroused or motivated. Too little or too much arousal impairs performance.

- Optimal arousal differs from skill to skill and from athlete to athlete.

- Athletes become anxious when they are uncertain about whether they can meet the demands placed on them when meeting these demands is important to them. The greater the uncertainty and the more important the outcome, the greater the anxiety.

- You can help alleviate athletes' anxiety by decreasing uncertainty and helping to reduce the importance of the outcome.

(Reprinted, with permission, from Martens, R., Christina, R.W.,
Harvey, J.S., and Sharkey, B.J. 1981, Coaching Young Athletes
Champaign, IL: Human Kinetics, p.62)

The role of the parent

Two good friends of the author, who are very experienced international coaches working with young children in gymnastics, have focused specifically on 'the role of the parent'. Their comments are valuable and are reproduced here.

Children need their own unique support structure of immediate family, social environment and school. They may also need someone involved in their chosen interest (which in our case is physical activity) to stimulate their senses during formative years. Together, such a collection of potential supporters will undoubtedly best serve the needs of the child. As the 'line managers' of their offspring, it is the parents who are expected to take the lead in forming such a team, and undoubtedly this is often the case in relation to home and school selection. But can parents provide meaningful experience in areas such as physical control of the body, appropriate movement experience, and skill learning? Do they know which activities are best suited to young children, or how to recognize when children are ready to cope with new pursuits?

Sometimes their decision is a reaction to peer pressure or to current vogues, sometimes it is influenced by constraints on quality time together as a family unit. Parents usually make decisions about activity selection on the basis of their participation interests, the local facilities and the complexities of transportation, rather than choosing what would be most beneficial to the children. Questions of who is best placed to provide the chosen experience also tend to dwell on qualification issues rather than on philosophy or principles. This is not the parents' fault, as the majority of information regarding early childhood activity does not often compare the values of contrasting experience, or it is written in literature which is read more by researchers than by parents or coaches. That is why practical information based on research into growth function and early learning is needed.

(Gervis and Brierley 1999, p.9)

Chapter 9

Meet Some 'Graduates' of the Program

John

John was unhappy. He was regularly bullied at school. The other children saw him knock over the furniture in class; they saw him struggle with his writing; they saw him struggle in PE; they saw him as different and thought that this was enough to justify bullying him. John's teachers tried to protect him but they could not be everywhere and the bullies got at John and made him very unhappy. John was bigger than the other boys and physically he could have defended himself, but he lacked self-confidence and when he was bullied he covered his head with his arms and took his punishment.

John was in a class of 30 children who completed the exercise program for six weeks. He worked hard and made excellent progress. At the start of the six weeks he was able to complete one set of ten bench jumps, but when he finished he complained that he was tired and that the muscles on the front of his legs and his lower back were tired, although he recovered fairly quickly.

After just six weeks, John was able to complete four sets of 100 bench jumps with just a 60-second recovery between each set. He no longer complained of feeling tired or of the muscles in his legs and back feeling tired. He enjoyed the exercise and he was pleased with his progress.

The week after the program ended I had to return to the school to meet the principal. I wanted to express my appreciation for her cooperation and feed back to her on the way that the program had gone. On my way to the principal's office I met John. He had a black eye and when I mentioned this to the principal she told me the story. Apparently, John's teachers had noticed a substantial improvement in John's writing and general movement skills. There had also been a consequential improvement in John's self-confidence and when he was targeted for another regular dose of bullying he had decided to defend himself and had seen off the bullies.

Whilst not condoning the use of violence in any way, I must admit to a certain degree of pride in being able to have such a fundamentally positive effect on John's ability to go through life without being bullied.

The program had been designed to eliminate movement difficulties but improving self-confidence is a natural consequence of improved movement skills and can have equally significant benefits for the affected child. I was told that John's improvement in movement skills and self-confidence was reflected in John's schoolwork and in his relationship with his fellow students.

Sophie

Sophie was four-and-a-half years old and she was in the reception class at her local primary school. She had movement difficulties. She could not use scissors to cut paper and when she tried to play with a jigsaw the whole thing landed on the floor. But the problems did not stop there.

When Sophie experienced problems in completing tasks, everybody else knew about it. She would throw things. She would scream. She would hit the nearest person. She would have a tantrum.

Sophie completed the program for six weeks. Being the daughter of middle-aged parents, she had not done much sport or exercise and she enjoyed the chance to stretch her legs and test herself against a class of her peers. She worked hard and the progress was clear for all to see.

It was in the classroom and not the gymnasium or the playing field that the biggest difference was noticed, however. Sophie experienced fewer movement difficulties. Her skills improved and there were fewer accidents and more successes. Life for Sophie's teachers and classmates became calmer and quieter. The outbursts and the tantrums stopped completely.

Not only was Sophie learning more, but so were all the other children in her class, who no longer had to tread carefully in Sophie's presence, fearful of a tantrum or outburst. They also no longer had to deal with all the distractions in class.

References

American Psychiatric Association (2000) *Diagnostic and Statistical Manual of Mental Disorders – Fourth Edition, Text Revision (DSM-IV-TR).* Washington DC: American Psychiatric Association.

Arnheim, D.D. and Sinclair, W.A. (1979) *The Clumsy Child: A Programme of Motor Therapy.* St. Louis, MI: C.V. Mosby and Company.

Ayres, A.J. (1972) *Sensory Integration and Learning Disorders.* Los Angeles, CA: Western Psychological Services.

BBC (2009) 'Child fitness levels declining even in affluent areas.' Available at http://news.bbc.co.uk/1/hi/health/8425161.stm, accessed 21 August 2014.

Baden-Powell, R. (1899) *Aids to Scouting: For N.C.O.s and Men.* London: Gale and Polden.

Baden-Powell, R. (1908) *Scouting for Boys: A Handbook for Instruction in Good Citizenship.* London: Stevens Publishing.

Baechle, T.R. and Earle, R.W. (2008) *Essentials of Strength Training and Conditioning.* Champaign, IL: Human Kinetics Publishers.

Bayley, N. (1969) *Manual for the Bayley Scales of Infant Development.* New York, NY: Psychological Corporation.

Behm, D.G., Faigenbaum, A.D., Falk, B. and Klentrou, P. (2008) 'Canadian Society for Exercise Physiology position paper: Resistance training in children and adolescents.' *Applied Physiology, Nutrition and Metabolism, 33,* 3, 547–561.

Bellman, M.H., Lingam, S. and Aukett, A. (1996) *Schedule of Growing Skills II.* Windsor: NFER-Nelson.

Berkey, C.S., Rockett, H.R., Field, A.E., Gillman, M.W. *et al.* (2000) 'Activity, dietary intake, and weight changes in a longitudinal study of preadolescent and adolescent boys and girls.' *Pediatrics, 105,* E56.

Biggs, V. (2014) *Caged in Chaos: A Dyspraxic Guide to Breaking Free.* London: Jessica Kingsley Publishers.

Blythe, P. (1992) 'A physical approach to resolving learning difficulties.' Paper presented at the 4th European Conference of Neuro-developmental Delay in Children, Chester.

Boon, M. (2002) *Helping Children with Dyspraxia.* London: Jessica Kingsley Publishers.

Boon, M. (2010) *Understanding Dyspraxia: A Guide for Parents and Teachers* (2nd edition). London: Jessica Kingsley Publishers.

Booth, S.L., Sallis, J.F., Ritenbaugh, C., Hill, J.O. *et al.* (2001) 'Environmental and societal factors affect food choice and physical activity: Rationale, influences, and leverage points.' *Nutrition Reviews, 59,* S21–S39.

Bouchard, C., Ping, A., Rice, T., Skinner, J. *et al.* (1999) 'Familial aggregation of VO2 max response to exercise training results from the Heritage Family Study.' *Journal of Applied Physiology, 87,* 3, 1003–1008.

Branta, C., Haubenstricker, J. and Seefeldt, V. (1984) 'Age changes in motor skills during childhood and adolescence.' *Exercise Sports Sciences Review, 12,* 1, 467–520. In Washington, R.L., Bernhardt, D.T., Gomez, J., Johnson, M.D., et al. (2001) 'Committee on Sports Medicine and Fitness and Committee on School Health, Organized Sports for Children and Preadolescents.' *Pediatrics ,107,* 6, 1459–1462.

British Medical Journal (1962) 'Clumsy children.' *British Medical Journal, 2,* 1665–1666.

Brookes, G. (2007a) *Dyspraxia (Special Educational Needs).* London: Continuum International Publishing Group Ltd.

Brookes, G. (2007b) *The Teaching Assistant's Guide to Dyspraxia.* London: Continuum International Publishing Group Ltd.

Bruininks, R.H. (1978) *Bruininks-Oseretsky Test of Motor Proficiency: Examiner's Manual.* American Guidance Service. ASIN: B0006CZOY4.

Chandler, T.J., Kibler, W.B., Stracener, E.C., Ziegler, A.K. and Pace, B. (1992) 'Shoulder strength, power, and endurance in college tennis players.' *American Journal of Sports Medicine, 20,* 4, 455–458.

Colley, M. (2006) *Living with Dyspraxia: A Guide for Adults with Developmental Dyspraxia.* London: Jessica Kingsley Publishers.

Collins English Dictionary. Glasgow: HarperCollins.

Cooper, R.A., Quatrano, L.A., Axelson, P.W., Harlan, W. *et al.* (1999) 'Research on physical activity and health among people with disabilities: A consensus statement.' *Journal of Rehabilitation Research and Development, 36,* 142–154.

Coster, W., Deeney, T., Haltiwanger, J. and Haley, S. (1998) *School Function Assessment.* San Antonio, TX: Psychological Corporation.

Crawford, S., Wilson, B.N., and Dewey, D. (2001) 'Identifying developmental coordination disorder: Consistency between tests.' *Physical and Occupational Therapy in Pediatrics, 20,* 29–50.

Croisier, J.-L., Forthomme, B., Namurois, M.-H., Vanderthommen, M., Crielaard, J.-M. (2002) 'Hamstring muscle strain recurrence and strength performance disorders.' *American Journal of Sports Medicine, 30,* 2, 199–203.

Davis, W.E. and Burton, A.W. (1991) 'Ecological task analysis: Translating movement behaviour theory into practice.' *Adapted Physical Activity Quarterly, 8,* 154–77.

Department of Education and Science (1980) *Safety Series No. 4.* London: Her Majesty's Stationery Office. In Hamill, B.P. (1994) 'Relative safety of weightlifting and weight training.' *Journal of Strength and Conditioning Research, 8,* 1, 53–57.

Dick, F.W. (2003) *Sports Training Principles.* London: A&C Black Publishers Ltd.

FSA (2009) 'Labelling and packaging.' Available at www.food.gov.uk/foodlabelling, accessed 21 August 2014.

Faigenbaum, A.D. and Westcott, W.L. (2000) *Strength and Power for Young Athletes.* Champaign, IL: Human Kinetics Publishers.

Faigenbaum, A.D., Kraemer, W.J., Cahill, B., Chandler, J. *et al.* (1996). 'Youth resistance training: Position statement paper and literature review.' *Strength and Conditioning Journal, 18,* 6, 62–75.

Farnham-Diggory, S. (1992) *The Learning Disabled Child.* Cambridge, MA: Harvard University Press.

Folio, M.R. and Fewell R.R. (2000) *Peabody Developmental Motor Scales.* Therapy Skill Builders.

Frankenburg, W.K. and Dodds, J.B. (1967) 'The Denver Developmental Screening Test.' *Journal of Paediatrics, 71,* 181–91.

Frankenburg, W.K., Dodds, J., Archer, P. and Bresnick, B. (1990) *Denver II Technical Manual.* Denver, CO: Denver Developmental Materials Inc.

Gallahue, D.L. and Ozmun, J.C. (1995) *Understanding Motor Development* (3rd edition) Madison, WI: Brown & Benchmark.

Gervis, M. and Brierley, J. (1999) *Effective Coaching for Children: Understanding the Sports Process.* Marlborough: Crowood Press.

Geuze, R. (2007) *Developmental Coordination Disorder: A Review of Current Approaches.* Marseille: Solal Editeurs.

Griffiths, R. (1970) *The Abilities of Young Children: A Comprehensive System of Mental Measurement for the First Eight Years of Life.* London: Child Development Research Centre.

Hadders-Algra, M. (2003) 'Developmental coordination disorder: Is clumsy motor behavior caused by a lesion of the brain at early age?' *Neural Plasticity ,10,* 39–50.

Haley, S.M., Coster, W.J., Ludlow, L.H., Haltiwanger, J.T. and Andrellos, P.J. (1992) *Pediatric Evaluation of Disability Inventory (PEDI): Development, Standardisation and Administration Manual.* London: The Psychological Corporation.

Hamill, B.P. (1994) 'Relative safety of weightlifting and weight training.' *Journal of Strength and Conditioning Research, 8,* 1, 53–57.

Haubenstricker, J., Seefeldt, V., Fountain, C. and Sapp, M. (1981) 'The efficiency of the Bruininks-Oseretsky Test of Motor Proficiency in discriminating between normal children and those with gross motor dysfunction.' Paper presented at the Motor Development Academy at the AAHPERD Convention, Boston, MA.

Haywood, K.M. and Getchell, N. (2005) *Life Span Motor Development.* Champaign, IL: Human Kinetics Publishers.

Heiser, T.M., Weber, J., Sullivan, G., Clare, P. and Jacobs, R.R. (1984) 'Prophylaxis and management of hamstring muscle injuries in intercollegiate football players.' *American Journal of Sports Medicine, 12,* 5, 368–370.

Henderson, S.E. and Sugden. D.A. (1992) *Movement Assessment Battery for Children.* London: The Psychological Corporation.

The Independent (2009) 'Ban on fast food outlets near schools.' Available at www.independent.co.uk/news/education/education-news/ban-on-fast-food-outlets-near-schools-969779.html, accessed 22 August 2014.

Kennedy, J.F. (1960) *The Soft American.* Speech by John F. Kennedy on 26 December.

Keogh, J.F. (1982) 'The Study of Movement Learning Disabilities'. In J.P. Das, R.F. Mulcahy and A.E. Wall (eds.), *Theory and Research in Learning Disabilities.* New York: Plenum Press.

Kirby, A. and Drew, S. (2003) *Guide to Dyspraxia and Developmental Coordination Disorders.* London: David Fulton Publishers.

Kolata, G. (2002) 'Why some people won't be fit despite exercise'. *New York Times*, 12 December 2002. Available at http://query.nytimes.com/gst/fullpage.html?res=946EEDE113CF931A25751COA9649C8B63&sec=health, accessed 22 August 2014.

Kraemer, W.J. and Fleck, S.J. (1993) *Strength Training for Young Athletes.* Champaign, IL: Human Kinetics Publishers.

Kurtz, L.A. (2008) *Understanding Motor Skills in Children with Dyspraxia, ADHD, Autism, and Other Learning Disabilities: A Guide to Improving Coordination.* London: Jessica Kingsley Publishers.

Laszlo, J.I. and Bairstow, P.J. (1985) *Kinaesthetic Sensitivity Test.* Perth, WA: Senkit PTY in association with London: Holt, Rinehart and Winston.

Lee, M.G. and Smith, G.N. (1998) 'The effectiveness of physiotherapy for dyspraxia.' *Physiotherapy, 84,* 276–284.

Lehmkuhle, K. and Williams, M. (1993) 'Defective visual pathway in dyslexics.' *New England Journal of Medicine, 328,* 989–995.

Livingstone, M.S., Rosen, G.D., Drislane, F.W. and Galaburda, A.M. (1991) 'Physiological and anatomical evidence for a magnocellular defect in developmental dyslexia.' *Proceedings of the National Academy of Science of the USA, 88,* 18, 7943–7947.

Loovis, E.M. and Ersing, W.F. (1979) *Assessing and Programming Gross Motor Development for Children.* Bloomington, IN: Tichenor Publishing.

Macintyre, C. (2002) *Dyspraxia in the Early Years: Identifying and Supporting Children with Movement Difficulties.* London: David Fulton Publishers.

Magill, R.A. (2003) *Motor Learning and Control: Concepts and Applications.* New York: McGraw Hill Education.

Martens, R., Christina, R.W., Harvey, J.S. and Sharkey, B.J. (1981) *Coaching Young Athletes.* Champaign, IL: Human Kinetics Publishers.

McClenaghan, B.A. (1976) *Development of an Observational Instrument to Assess Selected Fundamental Movement Patterns of Low Motor Functioning Children.* Unpublished Doctoral Dissertation, Indiana University.

McClenaghan, B.A. and Gallahue, D.L. (1978) *Observation and Assessment.* Philadelphia, PA: WB Saunders.

McCreight, B. (1997) *Recognizing and Managing Children with Fetal Alcohol Syndrome/Fetal Alcohol Effects: A Guidebook.* Washington DC: CWLA Press.

Nietzsche, F. (1888) *Twilight of Idols and Anti-Christ.* Reprinted in 2003 by Penguin Classics. London: Penguin.

Nordau, M.S. (1892) *Degeneration.* London: Heinemann Publishers.

Oliveira, M.A., Loss, J.F., Petersen, R.D.S., Clark, J.E. and Shim, J.K. (2006) 'Kinetic redundancy on hand digit control in children with DCD.' Available at www.asbweb.org/conferences/2006/pdfs/142.pdf, accessed 22 August 2014.

Orton, S.J. (1937) *Reading, Writing and Speech Problems in Children.* New York: Norton.

Pearson, D., Falgenbaum, A., Conley, M. and Kraemer, W.J. (2000) 'The National Strength and Conditioning Association's basic guidelines for the resistance training of athletes.' *Journal of the National Strength and Conditioning Association, 22*, 4, 14–27.

Piaget, J. (1962) 'Play, dreams, and imitation in childhood.' New York: W.W. Norton. In Rowland, T.W. (2007) 'Promoting physical activity for children's health.' *Sports Medicine, 37*, 11, 929–936.

Platt, G.K. (2010) 'Strength training as an intervention for children with DCD.' Unpublished doctoral dissertation. Edinburgh: University of Edinburgh.

Pollard, I. (2007) 'Neuropharmacology of drugs and alcohol in mother and fetus.' *Seminars in Fetal and Neonatal Medicine, 12*, 106–113.

Pomeroy, S.B., Burstein, S.M., Donlan, W. and Roberts, J.T. (2009) *A Brief History of Ancient Greece: Politics, Society and Culture.* Oxford: Oxford University Press.

Raynor, A.J. (1989) *The Running Pattern of Seven Year Old Children: Coordination and Gender Differences.* BPD Honours thesis. Nedlands, Australia: University of Western Australia.

Raynor, A.J. (2001) 'Strength, power, and coactivation in children with developmental coordination disorder.' *Developmental Medicine and Child Neurology, 43*, 676–684.

Roach, E.G. and Kephart, N.C. (1966) *The Purdue Perceptual Motor Survey (PPMS).* Columbus, OH: Charles E. Merrill Publishing Co.

Rowland, T.W. (2007) 'Promoting physical activity for children's health.' *Sports Medicine, 37*, 11, 929–936.

Rugby Football Union (1990) *6th Report on Injuries.* Twickenham: Rugby Football Union. In Hamill, B.P. (1994) 'Relative safety of weightlifting and weight training.' *Journal of Strength and Conditioning Research, 8*, 1, 53–57.

Sandercock, G., Voss, C., McConnell, D. and Rayner, P. (2010) 'Ten year declines in the cardiorespiratory fitness of affluent English children are largely independent of changes in body mass index.' *Archives of Disease in Childhood, 95*, 46–47.

Schmidt, R.A. and Wrisberg, C.A., (2008) *Motor Learning and Performance: A Problem-based Learning Approach.* Champaign, IL: Human Kinetics Publishers.

Schraw, G., Crippen, K.J. and Hartley, K. (2006) 'Promoting self-regulation in science education: Metacognition as part of a broader perspective of learning.' *Research in Science Education, 36*, 111–139.

Seefeldt, V. and Haubenstricker, J. (1976) *Developmental Sequences of Fundamental Motor Skills.* Unpublished research, Michigan State University.

Simeonsson, R.J., McMillen, J.S. and Huntington, G.S. (2002) 'Secondary conditions in children with disabilities: Spina bifida as a case example.' *Mental Retardation and Developmental Disabilities Research Reviews, 8*, 198–205.

Smith, A. and Biddle, S.J.H. (2008) *Youth Physical Activity and Sedentary Behaviour: Challenges and Solutions.* Champaign, IL: Human Kinetics Publishers.

State, O. (1955) *Weight Training For Athletics.* London: Amateur Athletic Association.

Steele, C.A., Kalnins, L.V., Jutai, J.W., Stevens, S.E., Bortolussi, J.A. and Biggar, W.D. (1996) 'Lifestyle health behaviors of 11- to 16-year-old youth with physical disabilities.' *Health Education Research, 11*, 173–186.

Stein, J. (2003) 'Visual motor sensitivity and reading.' *Neuropsychologica, 41*, 1785–1793.

Stone, M.H., Stone, M. and Sands, W.A. (2007) *Principles and Practice of Resistance Training.* Champaign, IL: Human Kinetics Publishers.

Stratton, G., Jones, M., Fox, K.R., Tolfrey, K. *et al.* (2004) 'BASES position statement on guidelines for resistance exercise in young people.' *Journal of Sports Sciences, 22*, 4, 383–390.

Sugden, D.A. and Wright, H.C. (1998) *Motor Coordination Disorders in Children. Developmental Clinical Psychology and Psychiatry*, vol. 30. London: Sage Publications.

Touwen, B.C.L. (1979) *Examination of the Child with Minor Neurological Dysfunction. Clinics in Developmental Medicine.* London: SIMP with Heinemann Medical.

Ulrich, D.A. (1985) *Test of Gross Motor Development.* Austin, TX: Pro-Ed. ASIN: B0006EMDCS.

US Department of Health and Human Services (1999) P*romoting Physical Activity.* Champaign, IL: Human Kinetics Publishers.

van der Ploeg, H.P., van der Beek, A.J., van der Woude, L.H.V. and van Mechelen, W. (2004) 'Physical activity for people with a disability: A conceptual model.' *Sports Medicine, 34,* 639–649.

Victor, J.D., Conte, M.M., Burton, L. and Nass, R.D. (1993) 'VEPs in dyslexics and normals: Failure to find difference in transient or steady state responses.' *Vision Neuroscience ,10,* 939–946.

Walker, B. (2004) 'The FITT Principle in relation to injury prevention.' Brian Mackenzie's Successful Coaching. Available at www.brianmac.co.uk/articles/scni15al.htm, accessed 22 August 2014.

Washington, R.L., Bernhardt, D.T., Gomez, J., Johnson, M.D. *et al.* (2001) 'Committee on Sports Medicine and Fitness and Committee on School Health, Organized Sports for Children and Preadolescents.' *Pediatrics, 107,* 6, 1459–1462.

WHO (1992) *The ICD-10 Classification of Mental and Behavioural Disorders: Clinical Descriptions and Diagnostic Guidelines.* Geneva: World Health Organization.

Wislett, U., Ellingsen O. and Kemi O. (2009) 'High-intensity interval training to maximize cardiac benefit of exercise training?'. *Exercise and Sports Sciences Reviews, 37,* 3, 139–146.

Zatsiorsky, V.M. and Kraemer, W.J. (2006) *Science and Practice of Strength Training.* Champaign, IL: Human Kinetics.

Subject Index

Sub-headings in *italics* indicate tables.

Author Index